how t
have y

best
year
ever

SOUND WISDOM BOOKS BY JIM ROHN

The Power of Ambition

The Art of Exceptional Living

Take Charge of Your Life

The Day that Turns Your Life Around

How to Have Your Best Year Ever

how to
have your

best
year
ever

strategies for growth,
productivity, & happiness

JIM ROHN

An Official Nightingale-Conant Publication

Published and distributed by:
SOUND WISDOM
P.O. Box 310
Shippensburg, PA 17257-0310
717-530-2122

info@soundwisdom.com

www.soundwisdom.com

ISBN 13 TP: 978-1-64095-489-2

ISBN 13 eBook: 978-1-64095-490-8

For Worldwide Distribution, Printed in the U.S.A.

1 2 3 4 5 6 7 8 / 28 27 26 25 24

CONTENTS

FOREWORD

There is a day, seemingly like any other, when everything changes. It's the day when you decide once and for all to walk a new road toward the goals that, until that fateful day, have only been misty dreams. It's the day when you say, "I've had it with living a life of poor health, an empty bank account, and broken promises." This is the day when you're suddenly filled with the resolve to do whatever it takes to finally live the life you have always known you are capable of living.

It's the day when you're filled with the awareness that time is precious, and with each day that passes by unnoticed, it is like releasing a helium balloon into the sky. Too soon, it will be a distant memory never to be seen again. It's the day you decide to seize every precious moment and make each one count.

This can be your best year ever—day after day after day of living the life you've always dreamed about.

At the young age of 25, Jim Rohn, master motivator and business philosopher, met his mentor, John Earl Shoaff, who introduced him to a unique business opportunity in the world of network marketing. Not only did Mr. Shoaff mentor Jim on the lessons of building a remarkable business, he mentored him on building a remarkable life.

Jim Rohn used the lessons he learned to turn away from a life of mediocre performance, broken dreams, and an empty bank account to incredible levels of wealth, both tangible and intangible by the age of 31. His classic wisdom in this book helps you do the same. Jim shares ideas in a way you have never heard before by discussing the simple yet dramatic events of his own life-changing day, which led to many best years ever.

While life-changing days can be a profound as choosing to never drink again or as simple as deciding to take a painting class, every life-altering day holds something in common—all involve an internal battle inside our head, a battle that must be won.

As the author says, to win the battle in your own mind, you must trust the law of averages, that circumstances will work in your favor, and that your efforts will be rewarded. There's an old and proven saying that *if you can't find the circumstances you want, it's up to you to make them.*

Jim Rohn expands on this idea by showing you how to take action toward changing any area of your life for the better.

The key is to begin.

Sincerely,

Nightingale-Conant Corporation

1

TIME AND MONEY

Time is more valuable than money. You can get more money, but unfortunately you can't get more time. If somebody asks you to spend your money, that's pretty easy, right? Like me, you may live in the United States of America; we're wealthy compared to many other countries, so money's not the problem.

But what if somebody asked you to spend a day with them? I'm sure you would have to think that over carefully. I wouldn't waste even one of my days. Not for anybody, not for anything. Once I understood how valuable each day is, I haven't wasted any.

I appreciate that you have chosen to make an investment today of your money and your time to read this book, It cost me many of my days to speak to the hundreds upon hundreds of people that resulted in this book. I don't need the money, but I do need time. And I am happy to share that with you now.

I'm offering you the value I have earned, and I want to make reading this book worth your time. I've invested time into it and you're going to invest time too. Let's get the most out of it—and I have no doubt you can look forward to your best year ever!

FROM HERE TO THERE

I grew up farm country, in the southwest corner of Idaho. In fact, my father still lives on the old homestead where I grew up. He'll be 89 on his next birthday, and he still hasn't retired. I'm proud of my dad, he's really something. I'm trying to get him to retire this year, at age 88.

I told my father, "What a good year to retire, when you're 88."

And he says, "Hey, talk to me in ten years about that. I might be ready."

His attitude set the stage for my future outlook on life.

I went to high school. I graduated. I went to college one year; but halfway through my second year of college, I decided I was smart enough so I quit. That was one of my major mistakes. I should have stayed in school, but I thought, *Heck, I'm smart enough to get a job. That's what life's all about, right? I'll get a job, pay my bills, work hard, stay out of trouble, keep my fingers crossed and hope for the best.* I figured I was at least prepared to do that, so I quit college and went to work. A little while later, I got married, got my little family going, and I'm out there doing what I thought was the best I could do.

But about age 25, I started to struggle. I had purchased a little more than I could conveniently pay for on time, and the creditors started calling saying, "Hey, you told us the check was in the mail. What's the deal?" I'm embarrassed by that.

I was also embarrassed that big-mouth me made lots of fancy promises to get married. I was way behind on those promises and was discouraged, wondering what to do. *Well, maybe I should go back to school.* One year of college, pretty short on an application, but tough to go back to school, especially when I had a family. I realized that the time to stay in school was when I was there. So I discounted that idea.

Then I thought, *Well, if I had my own business, that would be the way to go, but I'm short on money.* Too much month at the end of the money—if you've ever been there, that's where I was at age 25. So I had to discount that idea too.

Now I wondered, *Where do I go from here?* And then the miracle happened for me! Good fortune came my way. And who can explain the remarkable things that happen to you at a particular time. Sometimes it's just unexplainable. One of my friends said, "Hey, things don't just happen. Things happen just." That may be a good saying to underline: *Things don't just happen. Things happen just.* I was ready for good fortune.

A friend of mine had gone to work for Earl Shoaff, a very wealthy man, and he started telling me about Mr. Shoaff. One day, my friend said, "You have to meet this man I work for. He's wealthy, but he's easy to talk to and he's got a unique philosophy of life." And the more he kept talking about this man, the more I thought, *He's right, I've got to meet this man.*

Shortly after that, I met this remarkable and wealthy man, and I was impressed. I was so intrigued that within a few minutes I said to myself, *Even though I'm a farm boy from Idaho, I'd give anything to be like Mr. Shoaff. If I could just get around him and if he would teach me what to do, I would be willing to learn. I'm coachable.*

And realizing that opportunity became my good fortune. A few months later, Mr. Shoaff took a liking to me and hired me. I went to work for him and spent the next five years in his employ. And then unfortunately, he died at age 49. I had spent the last five years of his life with him—and began the first five years of my new life. I got to spend time with this remarkable man, and my dream came true.

Mr. Shoaff coached me. He taught me. He educated me about the books to read. He instructed me on the disciplines of success. He showed me the changes I needed to make in my language and personality to become the best I could be. What he shared with me during those five years literally changed my life; it turned my life around. His wisdom changed my income, changed my bank account, changed my future, changed everything about me. I've never been the same since that unique experience.

I wish he was still alive today to see this Idaho farm boy who made it to Dallas-Fort Worth and other major cities to speak before full-house, standing-room-only seminars. If he was alive, I'd call him and say, "You won't believe what's happening to me. I now share with other people what you shared with me. Their lives have been changed for the better—because of what you taught me."

TELLING MY STORY

Thirty-plus years ago, I was living a successful life in Beverly Hills, California. One day, a businessman friend said, "Jim, I'd like you to come and share your story with the service club I belong to, the Rotary Club. I know your story, 'Idaho Farm Boy makes it to Beverly Hills,' and I think my club members would love to hear it. Would you come tell your story at one of our breakfast meetings? Just share a few thoughts."

I agreed to give this breakfast talk, and guess what? They liked it. Then my telephone rang and rang, call after another call saying, "We heard about your story and the ideas you shared. Would you come talk to our club?" I agreed and not long after, I was devoting a piece of my business time to giving these talks.

Then one day, a businessman who had heard my talk two or three times approached me and said, "Would you come and share that story and some thoughts with my management salespeople?"

"Well, let me think about it. I have a little company going that needs my attention," I told him.

He said, "If you come tell your story to my organization, I'd be happy to pay you."

And I thought, *Wow, wouldn't that be something? To get paid for sharing what I know, what Earl Shoaff taught me?* So I agreed and I got paid. Little did I know another fortune was waiting for me to translate my ideas into talks and speeches and seminars and books. Now I get to travel around the world. Last year I was in Japan and Israel, Spain, Mexico, Australia, New Zealand, France, Germany, Canada, and across the United States.

It's almost too much for me to comprehend from where I started. Raised in obscurity in a small farming community—and now to be jetting around the world is pretty awesome for me. So that's just a little bit of my story, which may be more intriguing for me than it is for you, but I wanted you to hear it.

I don't ask you to be impressed, but that's the American dream come true. A chance to start from scratch, start from obscurity, start with pennies, start with nothing, and have the opportunity to transform your life.

Throughout these pages, I offer you strategies for growth, productivity, and happiness. You can absolutely change your life, set your goals, and see what you can accomplish. That's how it "happened just" for me, and I'm delighted that this day has arrived for you too. I truly want to help make your future as valuable as possible.

SINCERITY AND TRUTH, IDEAS AND INSPIRATION

Let's go to work. Here's what I hope you'll find in this book:

ONE: SINCERITY AND TRUTH

Above all else, I hope you'll find me sincere. Always the best place for people to start to communicate is with sincerity on both sides. I'm sure you're sincere or you wouldn't be reading this book, right? To spend money, to spend time, to roll up your sleeves and go to work to experience your best year ever means you must be sincere. So I presume you're sincere.

I want you to see me as sincere. Sincerity is not a test of truth. We must not make the mistake of saying, "He must be right. He's so sincere." That is a mistake, and here's why—it's possible to be sincerely wrong. So don't mistake sincerity for truth. Truth has to yet be tested by truth. Hopefully you will find me sincere and truthful.

Sincerity is not a test of truth. Truth has to yet be tested by truth.

TWO: IDEAS AND INSPIRATION

Ideas are infinite—business ideas, social ideas, personal ideas. We all need ideas to move us ahead in our careers, relationships, and personal aspirations. We all need how-to-have-a-good-day ideas, good-year ideas, your-best-year-ever ideas. Good health ideas, personal relationship ideas, dealing-with-your-family ideas, sales management and production ideas, financial-freedom-for-the-future ideas, and so on.

We all need good ideas. So I share as many ideas with you as I possibly can, and here's why: ideas can be life-changing. Sometimes, all you need is just one more in a series of good ideas.

Ideas can be, and most often are, life-changing

For example, ideas can be like dialing numbers into a lock. You dial in the first five or six numbers and the lock doesn't open. But you don't need five or six more numbers—maybe you just need one more. A sermon could open your good idea, the lyrics from a song could open it. The dialogue from a movie. A conversation with a friend.

That one last number you need to dial into the lock. That one last idea and the lock opens. There's the door for you to walk through, and maybe this book will furnish that for you. One more idea. I know you have had many ideas over the years— sometimes we have an impression, a thought that returns. I used to have those, but I only had that much going for me; I needed more. I needed what Earl Shoaff revealed to me.

And maybe all you need is just a few more thoughts, ideas to furnish you some ways and means to turn your life into the dream-fulfilled you want it to be. So this book is loaded with ideas—and inspiration. Who knows the mystery of inspiration, why some people are inspired and some are not? You were inspired to read this book, some were not. Who knows the mystery of why some people are inspired to further their careers, to learn more, to take advantage of opportunities, and some are not. This is what I call the mysteries of the mind, and I just leave it at that. Some things I don't try to figure out.

MOCKERS AND BELIEVERS

There is a very interesting story about the day the Christian Church was started.[1] I don't claim to know all there is to know about the Bible, but I do know it has changed the lives of millions worldwide for more than two millennia. One of the most classic presentations, or enduring sermons of all time was recorded back then. This teaching brought together a lot of people—more than 3,000 gathered to hear what was to be said.

What makes this story most intriguing is that when the sermon was finished, there was a variety of reactions to the same sermon. I find that fascinating. Some were perplexed, some didn't accept what was said, some mocked and laughed, and many believed. Why would anyone be perplexed with a good, sincere, straightforward presentation? Why would anyone mock or laugh at the truth that offered freedom from their bondage? Answer: because they are the mockers and the laughers. Simple as that. I used to try and figure out conundrums like that. For example, I used to say, "Liars shouldn't lie." How naïve I was. Of course they lie. They're liars—so they lie.

Speak to those you can inspire, encourage, and make believers.

As the story goes, the speaker was looking for the believers out of this multitude, and 3,000 believed. That's about as close as we can come to understanding the mystery. In every audience, some believe, some mock, some laugh, some are perplexed, and some don't know what's going on. That's the way it is. The way to be brilliant is to realize that in every audience you will encounter believers, mockers, and those who are perplexed. Speak to those you can inspire, encourage, and make believers.

BE THANKFUL

Another idea that will open locks within yourself and others is to be thankful. Be thankful for what you already have. That

Thanksgiving opens doors, windows, and the channels to growth, productivity, and happiness.

shouldn't be any problem in the United States of America, because everything we need is available.

For instance, people haven't worked and traveled the past 100 years to get into, say, Poland or North Korea. People don't say, "If I could just get to Syria, everything would be okay." No, everybody wants to come to America. Why? Everything's available here. All the books you need, all the churches you need, all the schools you need, all the instruction you need, all the inspiration you need, all the capital you need, all the markets you need, all the challenges you need, all the information you need, all the seminars you need. Everything's available here.

So, let's be thankful for what we already have. Thanksgiving opens doors, windows, and the channels to growth, productivity, and happiness. Give thanks and appreciate what you already have.

SQUELCH CYNICISM

What locks the doors and the channels to receive more? Cynicism. A cynic means you're inclined to be a pessimist, a skeptic, someone who distrusts and doubts.

When you are a cynic about the marketplace, people in general, institutions, relationships, your work, your abilities, and your opportunities, you lock away all the good things that are meant to be part of your life. Being a cynic about the past, current, and the future locks the door to advancement and prevents you from learning. Don't be a cynic.

Don't be a cynic.

BE A GOOD LEARNER

To learn and listen well is a challenge today. I understand that. It's hard to sit and focus specifically on one thing at a time. For instance, while reading this book, most of your life is still going on outside the words on these pages. Family, business, friends, the economy, politics, and whatever else is happening in the midst of your life pulls your attention away from your main focus.

Do the best you can to learn and listen well, to concentrate on what is most important at the time. Carve out time for learning. You will never be sorry.

UNDERLINE, CIRCLE, WRITE NOTES IN THE MARGINS

I encourage you to read this book with a pen or pencil in hand. Underline, circle, or star sentences or paragraphs that especially speak to you. Write some good notes in the margins. People still show me notes that they took years ago. One person told me, "I still use these notes I took 21 years ago to help me in my business and relationship with my family." I venture to say that the notes you take today will become that valuable for you, too.

One of the ways it pays off for me is for you to mark up the book, then use whatever makes sense. That's what I feast on, the stories that come back around. They confirm that it is worth me making the investment to spend a portion of my life, my time, and my energy sharing what I've learned. And I want this investment I'm making today to pay off in your tomorrows.

Of those who read this book, sure enough, six weeks from now, six months from now, six years from now, you will someday say, "What I read in that *Best Year Ever* book made me take action to make necessary changes in my life, my career, and in my family relationships." Knowing that makes the return worth it for me. Not the money. This is something you can't buy with money. When somebody says, "Thank you for touching my life and taking the time to make the investment," you'll realize that, indeed, the return on your investment is better than the money.

DON'T BE A FOLLOWER

Don't be a follower, be a student. I don't seek disciples. I have no movement for you to join. I'm sharing some of my experiences, good ideas, and good advice.

Therefore, I urge you to:

- Take advice, but not orders.
- Use information, but don't let somebody order your life.
- Do what is the product of your own conclusion; don't do what someone else says.
- Take what someone else says, process it, think about it, ponder it. If it makes you wonder, if it makes you think, then it's valuable.
- Take action, making sure that the action is not just what somebody told you to do. Make sure the action is the product of your own conclusion.

If you follow just some of those simple guidelines, the learning process can be swift and powerful. You can then apply that wisdom to your life, business, family, conversations, and equities of all kinds. Your growth, productivity, and joy in life will flourish and progress like mine did those first five years when I met a teacher willing to share with me. It turned my life around. I made significant life improvements that I am thankful for every day.

NOTE

1. See Acts 2:14-41 NLT.

2

LIFE'S FIVE PUZZLE PIECES

Some of what I learned between ages 25 and 30 from my teacher, Earl Shoaff, were the fundamentals. A few simple basics that, if you practice every day, can make all the difference in the world in how your life works out, how it all meshes effectively. I boiled it down to five major pieces of the life puzzle and how they all fit together.

ONE: PHILOSOPHY

Philosophy, in my personal opinion, is the major determining factor in how your life works out. To form your philosophy, you have to think, you have to use your mind. You have to process ideas. This whole process spans a lifetime, starting when you were a child with the schools you attended, your parents, your experiences—all that you processed by thinking helped develop your philosophy.

If someone would've asked me at age 25, "Mr. Rohn, why aren't you doing better in life by now? You only have pennies in your pocket, creditors are calling, you have nothing in the bank, and you're behind on your promises to your family. You live in America, you're 25 years old, you have a beautiful family, every reason to do well—yet you're not doing well. What's wrong?" It would not have occurred to me to blame my philosophy. It would not have occurred to me to say, "Well, I have this lousy philosophy, and that's why I only have pennies in my pocket and nothing in the bank, and things aren't working out." That would not have occurred to me.

I found it much easier to blame the government, much easier to blame high taxes. I used to blame the traffic, the weather, the circumstances. I figured that my future was tied to what everybody else was somehow in charge of, such as the economy and interest rates. I used to say things cost too much. That was my whole explanation—until my teacher taught me that the problem was my own personal philosophy.

Here's what's exciting about each person's personal philosophy—it's what makes us different from horses and birds and spiders and alligators. Our philosophy makes us different from all other life forms. The ability to think, the ability to use our mind, the ability to process ideas and not just operate by instinct.

You can order the entire process of your own life by the way you think, by exercising your mind. You can process ideas and come up with a better philosophy, a better strategy for your life, goals for the future, and plans to achieve those goals. All this comes from developing your philosophy.

Philosophy helps us process what's available. Once I got rid of all the excuses and started looking for ways to solve the real problem, which was me, my life exploded into change. My bank account changed immediately, my income changed immediately. My whole life took on a whole new look and

LIFE'S FIVE PUZZLE PIECES

**Humans
have the
unique ability**
to think,
to use our mind,
to process ideas—
**not just operate
by instinct.**

color immediately—and the early results I received from making these philosophical changes tasted so good.

I never stopped the process from that day on, and with a little refinement of your sail—by setting a better sail and refining your philosophy—your whole life can start to change from today on. You don't have to wait till tomorrow. You don't have to wait till next month. You don't have to wait till spring. You don't have to wait. You can start this whole process immediately. I highly recommend it.

JUDGMENT ERRORS

At the time of this writing, my father is 88 years old, he has never been ill, and he is still working. We had drilled a new well one day that provided extra water to get some more acres ready to use. He was all excited. That evening, my father was eating what he called his "midnight snack," a little bite to eat before going to bed. Guess what he had on his plate. An apple, a few Graham crackers, and a glass of grapefruit juice. I said, "No wonder you're so healthy."

My mom taught good health practices to all of us. I've never been ill, and I passed the big 50 sometime ago. My two daughters, ages 32 and 33, have never been ill. My grandkids, never been ill. The legacy marches on.

As I watched my father eat his midnight snack, suddenly it occurred to me that "an apple a day keeps the doctor away," as the age-old saying goes. What if that's true? You may think, *Well, Mr. Rohn, if that's true, that would be easy to do.* Then what's the problem? Why doesn't everyone have an apple a day and be healthy? Because it's easy *not* to do. It's easy not to adopt an apple a day as your own personal philosophy.

A few good choices repeated every day leads to health and wealth.

It's easier to adopt what the guy says on television, "A Snickers really satisfies!" You have to have a different philosophy to even care that an apple a day is healthier for you.

If you make that kind of an error in judgment every day for six years, it accumulates into physical disaster. Sometime the first year you say, "Well, I'm so healthy now. What difference is one candy bar going to make?" You must be smarter than that. Just because disaster doesn't fall on us at the end of the first day doesn't mean disaster isn't coming. You have to be smart enough to look down the road and say, "Will the errors in my present philosophy, in my judgment, cost me my good health in one year, six years, one month, six months?"

You have two formulas to choose from:

A few errors in judgment repeated every day **leads to failure.**

- The formula for failure is *a few errors in judgment* repeated every day for one month. This starts the disaster process.
- The formula for success is *a few simple disciplines* practiced every day. This starts a process for a whole new healthy, happy life.

A few simple disciplines practiced every day begins the process of turning your life around. If you continue the process to improve your health habits, money habits, communication habits, management habits, and all other habits, replacing each bad habit with good disciplines, you can immediately reap the benefits.

So that was the first of the five pieces of life—your philosophy.

TWO: ATTITUDE

We're affected by attitude, how we feel about the past and the future. You have to have a good attitude about the past. Use your past as a lesson to teach you, not a club to beat yourself with about your past falls, failures, or losses. Attitude is also how you feel about the future.

The promise of a better future is an awesomely powerful force to affect your life every day. Without a future well-designed, we take hesitant steps. Without goals, you may be timid, driven into a corner, not boldly willing to go and take your portion, take your share.

Your attitude reflects how you feel about people. You should have a good attitude towards others because it takes everybody to make a healthy family, business, corporation, community, state, and nation. It takes all of us to make a dynamic economy. It takes others to make the churches. It takes all of us to make the possibilities become realities. All the gifts that have flowed in our great country during the past 250 years are unprecedented in history. There's been nothing like it.

The different people with their gifts and talents and skills and inventions and work ethics—all of it mixed together made the United States of America. To miss the value of all that by some warped attitude about other people means you missed what this country stands for. When you have an appreciation for all citizens, you draw from all the goodness that has been blended together here for 250 years for your value and benefit. Think of what you can do with all that you have access to for each day in your business, your conversation, and for your resources. You can transform your life to an incredible degree.

Your attitude reflects how you feel about people— good and bad.

Your attitude also reflects how you feel about yourself. Understanding self-worth is the beginning of progress. Self-worth should be easy. If one of us can do it, all of us can do it. If anybody can think it, we all can think it. I can read, you can read. I can understand, you can understand. From where I came from, the few simple things I did and tried revolutionized my life in five years—you can do it too. Change pennies to fortunes. Change nothing to something. Change from being broke to being rich. If any of us can do it, we all can do it. That's the value you should place on yourself.

THREE: ACTIVITY

The third puzzle piece is the work part, taking action, and the activity is the miracle-working piece of life. We don't

What performs a miracle of increase **is putting wisdom and attitude into discipline, into labor.**

quite understand how a miracle works, but it doesn't mean it won't work. Miracles work. I'm an amateur on God, but my best analysis is that when God says, "If you'll plant the seed, I'll make the tree," I believe it.

I like that arrangement; God has the tough end of the deal. What if I had to make the tree? I'd be up late every night trying to figure out how to make a tree. Thankfully, the mystery and the miracles have already been set up. God says, "I provide the miracles. The seasons, the sunshine and rain. I've arranged all that. I just need somebody to plant the seed." You don't have to rub a crystal and sleep under a pyramid. Forget all that. Realize the miracle of your part in the process.

Activity is discipline—gaining wisdom from your philosophy and inspiration, the strengthening of attitude and faith and courage, commitment. If you take these two qualities— philosophy and attitude—and invest into activities, you can experience a miracle. Anything short of that, no miracle. Wisdom doesn't perform a miracle; attitude doesn't perform a miracle. What performs a miracle of increase is putting wisdom and attitude into discipline, into labor. And this labor now can perform a miracle.

There are two parts to the labor: *1) Do what you can; 2) Do the best you can.* I can't give you better advice than that. Let's look at each part.

1. DO WHAT YOU CAN.

To do what you can, ask yourself:

- *What am I not doing that could greatly change my health and wealth?*

- *What am I not doing that I should and could be doing?*
- *What am I neglecting to do that would be easy to do—that would increase miracle opportunities?*

Answer those questions as each relates to you personally. You don't have to put the answers on a public bulletin board, this is all just for your introspection. From the walk around the block to the apple to what to do with your money—these are important aspects of living your best year yet.

If you place a few simple disciplines into your philosophy of life, you will experience wealth beyond imagination. And if you include the activity part, the miracle-working part, the miracle will take care of itself.

When you hand a problem to a miracle worker, what would they be inclined to say? "No problem." I encourage you to hang out with folks like that. I belong to a small group like that. We do business around the world. When I hand these guys a problem, they say, "No problem." Really? How many books would they read to solve it? As many as it takes. How early would they get up to work on the problem? As early as it takes. How much information would they gather? As much as they needed. So it's what? No problem. Hang out with folks like that.

According to the Bible, Jesus was a miracle worker. When presented with paying a tax, He told His disciple, Peter, to go fishing. Peter was a fisherman, so he knew how to fish. If you know how to fish and you could fish, and yet you don't fish, there will be no miracle. You could change, you should change—but when you won't change, accumulated disaster follows. Could, should, and won't lead to disaster. But if you start the process of change—could, should, and will put it into action—the miracle belongs to you.

Jesus said to Peter, "Go down to the lake and throw in a line. Open the mouth of the first fish you catch, and you will find a large silver coin. Take it and pay the tax for both of us."1 That is a miracle.

First, get out that list you just wrote about what you could do and haven't done yet. Start cleaning up all those loose ends. This is the best place to start for personal change that will affect your bank account, affect your future, affect your income, affect everything. *You can't start a better life change process than doing what you should be doing.*

Don't postpone like other people postpone. Write or call that person who has been on your mind for days, weeks. Finish that project at work that you keep pushing aside. Take your spouse and kids to the park or zoo or wherever you promised to take them. You wonder, *Is it as simple as that?* The answer is *yes.* You don't need a pink package to fall out of the sky. You don't need a massive blast, or pre-conscious, subconscious mind-bending, or channeling, or finding a 2,000-year-old guru. You don't need any of that stuff. Pass on all that. Just *take action on what you know you can and should do.*

2. DO THE BEST YOU CAN BY SETTING UP DISCIPLINES.

If you do the best you can, you will set up disciplines in your life—and you will perform a miracle. If that's not your philosophy right now, I ask you to amend it. Let me give you one of the best pieces of advice from an ancient script: *Whatever*

You will create a miracle for your life if you:

1) Do what you can, and

2) Do the best you can.

your hands find to do, do it with all your might. Do it with all your strength and do it with all your power. What a good philosophy! Following that philosophy will revolutionize your life.

Contrary to that philosophy, a guy slips into his workplace late and slips out early. He stretches his morning break and lunch, and is the first one in the parking lot heading for happy hour. The company doesn't seem to notice. He tells his buddies, "Best as I can calculate, I'm putting in about a half day's work and I'm collecting a full day's pay. I got it made." He doesn't realize that he is sowing the seeds of his own disaster because of his own weak and distorted personal philosophy.

It's not the economy that determines your next six years. It's your philosophy about labor and about activity and about a miracle within your reach. It's your philosophy and your attitude and your ability to take action. All of that is called the process of life change, miracle-working. I encourage you to do what you can and do the best you can.

FOUR: RESULTS

The fourth puzzle piece is your results. Every once in a while you have to measure your progress in regard to your philosophy, attitude, and activity. That measure or evaluation is called results.

What are the results of your efforts at the end of the day, the end of the week? Don't allow too much time to go by without checking, without evaluating your progress. At the beginning of our mentoring relationship, Mr. Shoaff said to me, "In the past six years, how much money have you saved and invested?"

I said, "Zero."

He said, "You've messed up. How many books have you read in the last ninety days?"

I said, "Zero."

Not saving and not reading, I learned, is not how to get ahead in life. I had a lot more to learn.

With all the wisdom of the world available, you can absolutely:

- Change your life for the better
- Change your future for the best
- Develop any skill you need
- Earn the income you want
- Have all the treasures you want, the resources you want
- Have the relationships with your family you desire

Take this phrase to heart, "Results is the name of the game." What other game is there? We're asked in life simply to make measurable progress in reasonable time. After all, we demand it of our children. How many years do you want your child to spend in fourth grade? One. If it looks like they are not going to make it, we pour on legitimate pressure because of the lack of results.

Likewise, you yourself must expect to make measurable progress in reasonable time. Some aspects of your life you need to check every day, some at least by the end of each

Results is the name of the game.

week, every month, every first of January. Discipline is needed to take periodic progress measurements.

Employers expect you to make measurable progress in reasonable time as well. For example, a salesperson joins a company and is supposed to make ten calls the first week. It would be legitimate and wise to call him in on Friday and ask, "John, how many calls did you make this week?"

John says, "Well..." and he gives a long, sad story.

His employer says, "John, I don't need a story, I need a number. How many calls did you make this week?"

John was supposed to make ten calls. What if he made 20? What if he made one?

What do those numbers tell us about John's philosophy? Do they tell us something about his attitude? His disciplines? Of course. And if he wants a lesson in life change, all he has to do is be willing to face the numbers and come up with the results. That way, he can either celebrate the good results or fix whatever needs to be fixed in his disciplines—his philosophy, attitude, and activity.

The same is true for you. It is useful to measure your results or lack of. I believe in affirmations, which are valuable as long as you affirm the truth. As we have all heard, the truth will set you free. Free to do what? To help us amend our errors and absorb the disciplines that lead to positive life changes.

If you start with realizing that you have messed up, that is called progress. Step one is to see your current situation as a reality. It doesn't matter how small you start in the process of improving your life. When you instill one discipline at a time, one discipline feeds another, feeds another, and another, and you soon discover that your life is swept up in a whole cycle of positive motion. It's called life change. It's called income change. It's called health change, relationship with your family change.

Wealth of every kind—personal, financial, relational, physical—is waiting for you, if you don't curse what's available and start accepting what's possible to get the results you want.

Go for the numbers. For example, how many pounds overweight should you be at age 50? None. Yet John says, "I got big bones," and he's up about 20 pounds over his ideal weight. There should be a blinking light going at home and at work to remind him of the wrong number. Now he's up 35, 40 pounds. Red lights are blinking and a siren is blaring because his cholesterol numbers are almost out of control. Success is a numbers game in all walks of life.

I strongly encourage you to start checking your numbers. How many books have you read in the last 90 days? Transform your life, become cultured, powerful, mature, healthy, influential, all that makes life enjoyable. How many books, how many classes, how committed are you to taking what's available and turning it into wealth in every aspect of your life? When you pick up the process of generating the best results, your life will change to levels of the best order.

FIVE: LIFESTYLE

Lifestyle is simply learning how to live well, which is the last of the five major puzzle pieces of life. Here is our ultimate challenge. I've worked on this puzzle piece extremely hard since age 25. Now, after applying better philosophy, attitude, and activity, and then adding up the results, I've enjoyed a mighty good lifestyle.

Success is a numbers game.

What do you do with your results? This is the ultimate challenge—you must *fashion your results into a lifestyle*. You need to fashion for yourself what we call the "good life." The good life means different things to different people.

You must take your results—your money, the return, the assets you've gathered—and then fashion for yourself a lifestyle as if you are weaving a tapestry. Your very own tapestry of all that a good life means to you.

NOTE

1.   Matthew 17:27 NLT.

3

PERSONAL PROGRESS

Some of what Mr. Shoaff taught me came quickly, and some things came easily. Setting goals, that was easy; we discuss that in another chapter. What was hard to come to terms with and I had to struggle with was personal development. It was hard for me to give up my life-long blame list. It was so comfortable blaming the government and blaming my negative relatives and the company, company policy, unions, wage scale, economy, interest rates, prices, circumstances, and all that.

That list of excuses was difficult for me to give up, and it was quite a transition for me to put the blame where it really belonged—on myself. Mr. Shoaff started out by telling me something very, very important.

He said, "It's not what happens that determines the major part of your future. What happens, happens to us all. The key is what you do about it." To start the process of change, do something different for the next ninety days, such as reading books. Do something different, such as start a new health discipline, or start a new routine with your family. No matter how small, if you start doing different things with the same circumstances, you can make this your best year ever. Many

What you have right now is what you have attracted **because of the person you are.**

times we can't change our circumstances, but we can change ourselves to the betterment of ourselves and our family. We can change what we do and how we react."

Then Mr. Shoaff gave me another secret to success: "What you have at the moment, Mr. Rohn, you've attracted by the person you've become." These are just a few little simple principles that teach a lot. Once you understand these principles, these strategies, they explain so much about how you can have your best year ever.

Sometimes it's a little tough to blame yourself instead of the marketplace or the government or the weather. Taking responsibility instead of putting it off on someone or something else can be daunting. That transition can be a challenging mission. And this one was a little tough for me.

He said, "Mr. Rohn, you have only pennies in your pocket. You have nothing in the bank. The creditors are calling. You're behind on your promises. All that occurs because up until now, you've attracted these situations because of the person you are."

I said, "How can I change all that?"

He said, "Very simple. If you change yourself within, everything will change. You don't have to change what's outside. All you have to change is what's inside. To have more, you simply have to become more. Don't wish it was easier. Wish you were better. Don't wish for fewer problems, wish for more skills. Start working on yourself to make these personal changes— and all of life will change for you."

BETTER AND BETTER

So let's take a chapter to look at personal progress, or personal development. That's an extraordinary adventure I started at age 25—and am still adventuring, getting better and better. I want my craft to get better, my business operations to get better, everything I do to get better.

When I understood this simple formula, it was easy to figure out where the problem was, and I could go to work on solving it.

When discussing personal development, I always start with money. Money isn't the only place to start; it certainly isn't the only value, but money is easy to measure. To see if there may be some errors in your judgment and lack of disciplines in your life, we might as well start with money, because it's so easy to count. So let's just start there and see whether or not maybe we have messed up.

MARKETPLACE MISTAKES

We get paid for bringing value to the marketplace, which is key to understanding economics. Marketplace can also be described as reality. It takes time to bring value to the marketplace, but we don't get paid for time. It's very important to understand that *we don't get paid for time.*

Mistakenly, someone says, "I'm making about $20 for working an hour." Not true. If that was true, you could just stay home and have them send your money. No, you don't get paid for the hour. You get paid for the *value* you put into the time—*you get paid for value.* Because that's true, these are key questions to ask yourself:

To earn more money in the same amount of time, become more valuable.

- Is it possible to become twice as valuable and make twice as much money in the same time?
- Is it possible to become three times as valuable and make three times as much money in the same time?

Are those two scenarios possible? Of course! All you have to do to earn more money in the same amount of time is to simply become more valuable.

In the USA, there is a minimum wage but no maximum wage. You can start at the bottom of the earning ladder and work your way up the ladder. The whole economic scenario of life is to start at number one, then step up to number two by becoming more valuable, then three, four, and so on.

The five richest people in America and their earnings as of September 2023[1] may shock you:

1. Elon Musk: $251 billion (Tesla, SpaceX)

2. Jeff Bezos: $161 billion (Amazon)

3. Larry Ellison: $158 billion (Oracle)

4. Warren Buffett: $121 billion (Berkshire Hathaway)

5. Larry Page $114 billion (Google)

One of the top earning executives in America in 2023 was the CEO of Disney at $31.6 million. Would a company pay someone for one year's work $31.6 million? Yes. If the CEO helped Disney make $2.35 billion.[2] Why that much money? Because he has become so valuable.

Okay, so why do some people get paid only minimum wage an hour? Because they are not as valuable to the marketplace. It is important to make that distinction—not as valuable to the *marketplace*. These individuals are most likely valuable family members, valued members of the community and church, valuable volunteers to a worthy charity—those kinds of values. But to the marketplace, which is another definition of reality, they aren't as valuable, so they aren't paid as much. Those are called the facts. That's how it is.

So how do people making minimum wage earn more money? Simple answer—they have to work harder to become more valuable.

Someone may say, "Well, I'll go on strike for more money." There's a major problem with that reasoning and attitude. You can't get rich by demand. Someone else may say, "Well, I'm waiting for a raise." I'd tell that person that it's easier to climb the ladder than to wait for a raise. Why not just become more valuable rather than wait for something that may never happen?

MARKETPLACE MIRACLES

The key to all advancement is becoming more valuable in the marketplace. Why would we pay someone $400 an hour? Because they are valuable to the marketplace. There is no reason you can't climb the ladder here in the USA—millions of people have.

Consider this example. If you work for McDonald's and haul out the trash, you will be paid minimum wage. If you whistle while you haul out the trash and do more than what is asked of you, you will be paid minimum wage plus a dollar more an hour. Your good attitude makes you more valuable. Then keep becoming more and more valuable. Do more than your job description says to do, more than your boss tells you to do—management will notice and you will move up the ladder.

I received a telephone call five years ago, and the company representative said, "We're ready to expand internationally, and we need some help. We have a project for you. We'll add some millions to your fortune and make it worth your while."

I said, "Okay." A little later I thought, "Isn't that interesting that they called me? My next thought was, "Of course they called me. Who else would they call? They know I can get the job done." Why did I receive a telephone call worth millions? I had become valuable.

BECOME VALUABLE

As you know by now, I'm a farm boy from Idaho, raised in obscurity with only one year of college, and made all kinds of mistakes. Yet I receive a telephone call worth millions. How did that happen? I changed. I turned my life around. Is it possible for you to become that valuable? Yes.

"The secret," Mr. Shoaff said, "is to work harder on yourself than you do on your job." After I added that vital secret to my life philosophy, it turned my life around. He said, *When you work hard on your job, you make a living. But when you work hard on yourself, you can make a fortune.*" Wow.

At age 25, you would've said of me, "Jim Rohn's a hard worker," because it was true. I'm the guy who didn't mind getting to work a little early and staying a little late. But you

Work harder on yourself than you do on your job.

would probably also have said, "Even though Jim's a hard worker, he only has pennies in his pocket and nothing in the bank and he's behind on his promises." Well, that was true too. I was a hard worker, but I was working hard on my job—not on myself.

If you learn that simple but extremely significant principle and start the process of personal development to make yourself more valuable to the marketplace, you can dynamically change your financial well-being as well as every aspect of your personal life. Start today working harder on yourself than you do on your job.

Work hard on yourself and develop the skills you need to succeed. Work hard on yourself and develop the graces you need to create opportunities. Work hard on yourself to become more valuable to the marketplace. Your whole life can explode into phenomenal changes that bring promotions, value, connections, beneficial relationships, and more. Becoming more valuable to the company, no problem. Money, no problem. Economics, no problem. Future, no problem if you go to work on the inside.

Let the miracle of everything that's available to you work for you—start working on yourself to:

- Improve your philosophy.
- Turn your attitude from negative to positive.
- Project a pleasant personality.
- Enrich your language.
- Use your gift of communication to the fullest.
- Develop all your abilities and skills.

Develop your skills and graces that lead to value in the marketplace and at home.

When you make these personal changes, your life will become more satisfying and enjoyable than you have ever imagined it could be.

FOUR MAJOR LIFE LESSONS

Another scenario of personal development is four major lessons, based on the assertion that *life and business are like the four seasons.* Following that assertion gave me one of the key phrases that helped change my outlook on life: *I can't change the seasons, but I can change myself.*

At 25 years old, my best hope was to go through the day with my fingers crossed, saying, "I sure hope things will change. I sure hope things will change." It seemed to be my only way for my life to get better—if *things* would change. Here's what I discovered: nothing will change unless I do.

I can give you the shortest humans-on-earth history lesson in one sentence: opportunity mixed with difficulty. That's about as simple as I can put it. And opportunity mixed with difficulty will only change when you do. When you change, everything will change for you—your bank account, income, and future will change. The ability to acquire your dreams will change. It all changes if you change.

You may be thinking, *Well, Mr. Rohn, a lot of this stuff is fairly obvious.* That's true, but many people need somebody like me to come along and remind them, remind you. I have no new truth for you to discover. This is all timeless, ageless truth. And you may just need to hear it again so you will be motivated enough to take action.

LESSON 1: HANDLE THE WINTERS.

Winter comes right after autumn—every year, according to written history, for the past thousands of years. To cross your fingers and say, "I hope. I hope. I hope it doesn't come," is naïve and futile.

There are all kinds of winters, not just the cold and blustery weather winter of the season. There is also the winter downtime, the discouraging time. One writer called it a winter of discontent. There are winters when you can't figure out life, and the winter when everything seems to go wrong. There are economic winters, social winters, political winters, and personal winters. There are winters when your heart is smashed into a thousand pieces, and the nights are unusually long. These are wintertimes.

Barbra Streisand sings, "It used to be so natural to talk about forever, but used-to-be's don't count anymore, they just lay on the floor until we sweep them away. ...You don't sing me love songs. You don't bring me flowers anymore." A song of winter. We're all acquainted with those winter scenarios. We've been through them all.

What do you do about the winters? You can't get rid of January by tearing it off the calendar, but here's what you *can* do with the upcoming winters of your life. You can get wiser and stronger and better. That is a great list of good words to sear into your mind: *wiser, stronger, and better.* Challenge yourself before the upcoming winters of your life to become wiser, stronger, and better!

Wiser: Read more books. Listen to books and podcasts. Watch educational documentaries. Visit museums and libraries.

Take a few classes online or at your local community college. Anyone who wants to get wiser can absolutely do so.

Stronger: Like becoming wiser, anybody can get stronger. If you're willing to do the pushups, you can get physically stronger. If you're willing to practice your talents and improve your skills, your value will become stronger. Can you get stronger when handling life situations? Of course, but you have to go to work on yourself—your attitudes, choices, outlook. Don't blame anything or anyone else while wishing life was easier; rather, wish you were stronger and then take action.

Better: And anybody can get better—better at communicating, learning, helping, working, sharing, earning, everything. I've been lecturing now for 33 years, and the first time I gave a talk, I stood up and my mind sat down. I opened my mouth and nothing came out for quite a while. My knees were banging together, sweat poured off my face, and I was shaking like a leaf. But I got through it and I did it again and I got better and better every time I spoke. Now I can easily lecture for a few hours at a time. Don't waste time wishing away the winters—handle them head-on.

LESSON 2: TAKE ADVANTAGE OF THE SPRING.

Spring always follows winter. Spring offers opportunity—and you must take advantage of every opportunity. Don't miss the process of taking advantage of opportunities when they appear. Learn to plant in the spring, or beg in the fall. There is a certain urgency regarding springtime because only a handful of springs are offered to each of us. So take advantage swiftly and quickly. Don't let the time and opportunity pass you by.

Seize the day. Seize the moment. Seize the opportunity. Seizing what is available to you is key. Elton John sings, "She lived her life like a candle in the wind." Life is fragile, it's brief. Whatever you're going to do, do it, get at it today. Don't let good prospects and possibilities pass away without taking time for a chance to grow into a springtime full bloomer.

LESSON 3: SUMMERTIME IS TO NOURISH AND PROTECT.

There are two personal development challenges in the summertime: 1) to become capable, powerful, and wise enough to nourish what's good, and 2) to defend yourself against what's bad. You must learn to nourish and defend. Summertime holds the possibility of harvest time, but there is also the possibility of devastation. Sure enough, as soon as you plant your garden, the bugs and weeds come to try and ruin all your hard work.

A word of advice: bugs and weeds come in all sorts of disguises and will devastate your garden unless you prevent it. You have to nourish your valuable values like a mother, and go after the threat like a father. Nourish your garden and kill the weeds and bugs. Summertime is a challenging time. Summertime is a unique, complex mix of positive and negative, opportunity and threat.

What a scenario of life itself: Opportunity and threat to the opportunity, and you must deal with both wisely. You have to handle whatever threatens you. Don't let the weeds wreck your chances for a good harvest. Deal with your enemies in the summers of good and evil. The great struggle in life is called good and evil—tyranny and liberty, sickness and health, and on and on. It's the way life is.

Part of the personal development challenge is to learn how to nourish all of your values, from a garden to a family relationship, to a marriage, to a business. Whatever you value, nourish it, feed it, take care of it—and just as important, defend it. This is the way things are in summer.

LESSON 4: REAP THE HARVEST WITHOUT COMPLAINT.

You are responsible for the abundant harvest of a healthy personal development season—as well as a season that may lack the expected fruit. In both scenarios, you must reap the harvest without complaint. Take full responsibility for the outcome. Realize that it's not the seed, it's not the soil, it's not the sunshine, it's not the rain, it's not the miracle of life, and it's not the seasons to be criticized. We must take personal responsibility for the harvest—be it good or not so good. It's your crop, your responsibility. No complaints, no excuses.

One of the best indications of human maturity is when you realize that *no apology is expected if you've done well, and no complaint if you haven't done well*. That truth is where the answers lie within and without in the miracle of the possibilities that you have to work with.

PHYSICAL DEVELOPMENT

A few more points about personal progress and development include the physical side. It's essential to *take care of yourself, your physical body*. Do not neglect your physical self, your well-being. As mentioned previously, mother studied nutrition, and she passed along her wisdom to my father and to me, and I passed it along to my children and my grandchildren. What a legacy that was and is! And now I'm passing it along to you—learn to take care of yourself.

Some people don't do well in life because they don't feel well. They have the gifts and the skills, but they just haven't taken care of themselves enough to take advantage of all that a healthy body means. They don't have the vitality—and vitality is a major part of success.

I know a guy who raises racehorses. He feeds these horses better than he feeds himself. He's so careful about what they eat, and they are magnificent animals. They can run like the wind. But this guy can hardly walk ten steps up a flight of stairs before he's out of breath. The guy takes much better care of his animals than he takes care of himself. Some people feed their dogs better than they feed their kids. Nutrition, and a good diet are very important to maintain good health.

There are various aspects of the physical part of us. Our appearance is part of the physical. As you have no doubt heard, we never have a second chance to make a first impression. And here's some of the best advice on appearance I can give you, "God looks on the inside. People look on the outside."[3]

You may be thinking, *Well, people shouldn't judge you by how you look.* Well, let me tell you right now, they do. You can't deal in shoulds and shouldn'ts. You'll be tripped up the rest of your life. Of course, when people get to know you, they'll judge you by more than what they see. But at first, they will look you over. So here's the best advice I can give you—make sure the outside—the physical side—is a major reflection of what's going on inside.

Make sure your outside is an accurate reflection of what's going on inside.

Take a few minutes each day to look and feel your best. Shower, comb your hair, wear clothes that fit, eat healthy foods, exercise. Stay healthy and you will have your best year ever—year after year!

SPIRITUAL DEVELOPMENT

Now, here's the next part of personal development, the spiritual part. Although I consider myself an amateur on the spiritual side, I do happen to believe that human beings are *more* than just an advanced life form, an advanced species of the animal kingdom. I do believe humans are a special creation.

That's just my personal belief and I don't ask you to buy it—but here's what I do ask you to buy. If you *do* believe in spirituality in any manner, my best advice is to study it and practice it. Do not neglect your values. Do not neglect your virtues. Don't let your beliefs go unstudied. Put time into spiritual development. Nourish your inside as an important part of your whole being. That's my best advice on the spiritual side.

MENTAL DEVELOPMENT

Along with the physical and spiritual aspects of personal progress, development is the mental part of yourself. The most complete personal development plan includes developing mentally as well. We must continually learn, study, grow, and change for the better. That's what schooling is all about, and human development takes time. Incredible amounts of time.

It's why it's important to take time to read books and listen to experts on a variety of subjects and specifically topics of your choice. For humans to become their best, it takes time—more than any other life form. For example, consider a newborn wildebeest in Africa. Guess how much time it has before it has to run with the pack so it doesn't get eaten by the lions. Only a few minutes. As soon as the little wildebeest is born, it tries to stand up, but falls down. Its mother nudges it, gets it to stand up again, but it falls back down.

Finally, on little shaky legs, it tries to nurse, but mother pushes it away. She moves away so it can't nurse. Her actions convey her innate response to save her young: *You can't nurse now. You have to develop strength now. The lions, the lions!* The newborn falls down again, gets back up, tries to nurse. Mother pushes it away. *No, you have to make your legs strong. You have not much time—not hours, not days, only minutes.* Wow.

But the human baby—even after 16 years, we're not sure the person will be strong enough to get out of harm's way. It takes us an unbelievable amount of time compared to the wildebeest. So we have to realize that it will take time for personal development, spiritual development, physical development, and mental development, which involves feeding and nourishing our mind.

Some people read so little that they have rickets of the mind. They couldn't give you a good, strong argument as to their own personal beliefs if you gave them an hour to do so. One of the challenges parents have is to get our kids ready to debate the major life issues of the day. They have to be ready to debate, to stand strong for what is right, for the values that matter.

Take for instance, that many have debated for decades about communism. Communism teaches that capital (personal earnings, resources) belongs in the hands of the state, the government. Communism teaches that people are too stupid to know what to do with their capital and that the all-knowing government needs to control all the resources and mete out as it sees fit. The people are only to meekly show up for their work assignments.

Is that right? No, not according to the 300 million-plus citizens in America. The United States was founded on the principle that the power in the government comes directly from the people.[4]

It's vital to be able to define your philosophy of life and defend it. If you can't defend your virtues and if you can't defend your values, you will easily and quickly fall prey to ideologies that are not in your best interest or the interest of your family and community. In addition to our learning and standing strong for what is right, we have to help our kids especially to be able to debate the major life issues, political issues, social issues, religious issues, spiritual issues, nutritional issues, economic issues, and all the issues that are valuable for us to build the best kind of life.

Each of the lessons, advice, and tips discussed in this chapter are designed to help you progress and develop all parts of you that lead to success.

NOTES

1. Devin Sean Martin, "The 2023 Forbes 400: The 20 Richest People In America," *Forbes,* October 3, 2023; https://www.forbes.com/sites/ devinseanmartin/2023/10/03/the-2023-forbes-400-the-20-richest -people-in-america/?sh=3c0982e8571f; accessed January 30, 2024.

2. A. Guttmann, "Global net income of the Walt Disney Company 2006-2023," *Statista.com,* December 15, 2023; https://www .statista.com/statistics/273556/net-income-of-the-walt-disney -company/#:~:text=The%20Walt%20Disney%20Company%20 generated%20a%20net%20income,U.S.%20dollars%20in%20 the%20fiscal%20year%20of%202023; accessed January 31, 2024.

3. 1 Samuel 16:7 NLT.

4. "What are the Principles of the US Constitution?" *American History,* June 5, 2017; https://worldhistory.us/american-history/what -are-the-principles-of-the-us-constitution.php; accessed February 3, 2024. This is just one of many informative websites that explain the principles of freedom and equality upon which the United States of America was founded.

4

YOUR WEALTH-
FILLED LIBRARY

To ready yourself mentally and develop the best philosophy so you can defend your virtues and your values, you need a good library—you need to read books. This is not a new strategy—successful men and women have a habit of reading, learning, and knowing what they believe.

Earl Shoaff got me started on building my library. One of the first books he recommended was *Think and Grow Rich* by Napoleon Hill. He said to me, "Doesn't that book and title intrigue you? *Think and Grow Rich.* Don't you have to read that book?"

I said, "Yes, sir." So I went and found that book in a used bookstore. That's where I had to start, in a used bookstore. I paid less than 50 cents for it—and I still have it. It's one of the rare hardback-cover editions. *Think and Grow Rich* by Napoleon Hill. Wow, Shoaff was right. And I recommend it highly as one of the books to get your library started. It'll change your life.

Any home worth more than $200,000 has a library. Why do you suppose that is? Doesn't that make you curious? What does that say about people with a nice house? You may think, *Well, I can't afford a $200,000 home.* It doesn't matter what size your home is. Take your present apartment, clean out a closet, call it your library, act intelligent, and start this process of growth like I did. Start building a library.

Your library will reveal that you are a serious student of:

- Life
- Health
- Spirituality
- Culture
- Uniqueness
- Sophistication
- Economics
- Prosperity
- Productivity
- Finances
- Sales
- Management
- Skills
- Values of all kind

Let your library show you're a serious student. Don't be a casual learner. Don't be a lazy learner.

Information is the key. Learning is the beginning of wealth. Learning is the beginning of health. Learning is the beginning of prosperity. Learning is the beginning of democracy, the beginning of freedom. Learning brings value and virtue. Start the learning process. Don't hesitate to gather books for your library that'll teach you and instruct you today and for years to come.

Some ideas in *Think and Grow Rich* inspired me incredibly, and helped me to change my life for the better. Now, I have to admit that there's some weird stuff in it too. But you can separate out the weird stuff. In fact, that's a key to all books. Don't be a follower, be a student.

Another book Shoaff recommended and that helped me become financially independent was *The Richest Man in Babylon* by George S. Clason. I used it for years as a textbook to teach teenagers how to be rich by the age 40 living in America, 35 if they were extra bright, and much sooner if they found a unique opportunity. I'm telling you the same thing.

Don't be a follower, be a student.

So I recommend that the foundation for your library includes these two excellent books to read: *Think and Grow Rich* and *The Richest Man of Babylon*. Start building your library.

The following are some books that belong in key sections of your library called "mental food"—or food for thought. These books will nourish your mind. It's so important to nourish the mind, just as it is good sense to nourish the body.

Nourishment needs to be well-balanced. You can't live on mental candy. Somebody says, "Well, I just read stuff that's positive." That's second-grade thinking; you have to move on from second grade. You can't just be inspired. You have to be taught. You have to be educated about various subjects.

I recommend reading *How to Read a Book* by Mortimer J. Adler. Adler was the Chief Editor of the New Encyclopedia Britannica, a good set of books to have in your library. I've read a lot of his books including the *Six Great Ideas*. *How to Read a Book* not only gives you excellent suggestions on how to get the most out of a book, he also gives you techniques on how to get the *best* out of a book. It's very good. Also in his book is a list of what he calls the best writings ever written, which I've used as a centerpiece for my library.

WELL-BALANCED MENTAL NUTRITION

A well-balanced library is essential. The following is some of that balance that I recommend.

HISTORY

We should all have a sense of history: American history, national history, international history, family history, political history. We all need a sense of history. Be a good student of history. A great book to read is *The Lessons of History* by historians Will and Ariel Durant. This brief book is only about 100 pages, but I'm telling you it's so well written you'll be as intrigued as I was. There are many excellent books on history—choose some to read and place in your library.

PHILOSOPHY

Will Durant also wrote a good book on philosophy, *The Story of Philosophy: The Lives and Opinions of the Greater Philosophers*. It lists a good rundown of the key philosophers of the last several hundred years, what they taught and some of the lives they lived. You might find it a little difficult, but hey, you can't just read the easy stuff. Key phrase to add here in parentheses (don't just read the easy stuff). You won't grow, you won't change, you won't develop. Tackle the more difficult stuff.

NOVELS

Novels are good to have in your library. Sometimes an intriguing story keeps our attention so that the author can weave in the philosophy he or she's trying to get across. Ayn Rand was probably better at that than anybody else I could possibly think of. *Atlas Shrugged* is one of her towering novels. The novel keeps the reader intrigued, but guess what she was doing all the time? Feeding us her philosophy. Now whether you agreed with her philosophy or not, you will have to admit she was really good at getting it out there, weaving it through the story in the dialogue and in the speeches and in the text. Fabulous.

Now, here's a little personal advice about novels. Skip the trash. Somebody says, "Well, sometimes you can find something valuable in a trashy novel." Personally, I wouldn't read it to find it. You can find a crust of bread in the garbage can, but I wouldn't go through it to find it. For one thing, you don't need the reputation. Use your time to read the brilliant stuff, the good stuff, and skip the trash. My personal advice on personal development is to become more valuable than you are already—reading trashy novels won't do that for you.

BIOGRAPHIES AND AUTOBIOGRAPHIES

Read the stories of successful people, and unsuccessful people. There's some dramatic stuff that happened to people over the past 100-plus years, and much of it is very interesting. You need a book on Gandhi. You need a book on Hitler. One to illustrate how high a human being can go, and the other one to illustrate how low and despicable a human being can become. We need to read about both sides of life's scenarios. We need to see the balance.

THE BIBLE

The Bible is a unique book because it contains human stories on one side of the ledger as good examples for us, while on the other side of the ledger are stories that serve as warnings. The examples in the Bible say, "Look at these people's lives. Follow them, follow their philosophy, follow their advice." As well as, "Don't do what these people did. They messed up and threw their life away." Vitally important, both sides of the scenario. Now, if your life story ever gets in a book, make sure it's being used as an example, not a warning.

ACCOUNTING

Your library also needs to have at least a primary view of accounting. You need to know the basics, especially if you plan to create a business. Kids have to learn the difference between a debit and a credit. And you need to know how not to spend more than you make. Maintaining a balanced budget is highly recommended.

LAW

You don't have to be a lawyer, but you have to know about contracts, what to sign, what not to sign, and basic good advice. Know how to be safe rather than sorry; everyone needs to know the law and how it pertains to us.

I learned this lesson the hard way. A company wanted to borrow money, and the bank said, "Well, yes, we will loan the company the money if Mr. Rohn will sign personally." I wanted to play hero, and I knew the company could pay back the quarter of a million dollars. So I signed, no problem. Sure enough, within less than a year, they paid it all back. I am now a hero.

Well, about a year later, this company gets into financial trouble. They go back to the bank and borrow a quarter of a million dollars again. I thought, *I hope my phone doesn't ring, because I won't sign the note this time,* because I knew they were in trouble. I knew they were probably going to go bankrupt. My phone never rang. *I'm off the hook.* Sure enough, within less than a year, the company goes bankrupt and can't pay.

Then I get a letter from the bank saying, "Dear Mr. Rohn, since the company cannot perform its obligation to pay the quarter of a million dollars, and since we have here your personal guarantee, would you please send us your check for a quarter of a million dollars?"

I responded, "Hey, hold it. Hold it. There must be some mistake. I signed the first note and they paid it all back. I would not have signed the second note. I didn't sign the second note." Well, what I didn't know was that what I had originally signed was a continuing guarantee. So now I know what the word *continuing* means.

So, I'm highly recommending that you study enough law so that you know what to sign, and know how to defend yourself. Be a student of various aspects of life.

ECONOMICS

Be a student of economics, which teaches you about businesses, markets, governments, goods and services, and standards of living. Knowing some aspects of economics allows you to understand and make good decisions regarding managing your resources.

CULTURE AND SOPHISTICATION

Culture is part of the fabric of the nation. Culture is what makes us different from dogs and animals and barbarians. Culture and sophistication includes being a student of the arts and music and all the rest of those extraordinary human values that are possible for us all to participate in as well as to enjoy. Be a student of culture, defined as customary beliefs, social forms, and material traits of a racial, religious, or social group, including language, rituals, and ideas.

SPIRITUALITY

Study spirituality in the Bible. There are many related books about spirituality. If you're a believer, study and practice. Let your library show you're a serious student.

KEEP A JOURNAL

Next, keep a journal. Earl Shoaff said, "Mr. Rohn, not only be a student, but record the good ideas that you develop from the books. Keep a separate journal. Write down everything." He said, "Don't trust your memory. If you're serious about becoming wealthy and powerful and sophisticated and healthy, influential, cultured, and unique, keep a journal. Don't trust your memory."

If you listen to something valuable, write it down. If you come across something important, write it down. I used to take notes on pieces of torn-off corners and backs of envelopes and restaurant placemats and long sheets and narrow sheets and little sheets and pieces that get thrown in a drawer. Then I found that the best way to record my notes is to keep a journal. I've been keeping journals since age 25. Journaling makes up a valuable part of my personal learning, and each journal is a valuable part of my library. Over the years, my own journals now form a good portion of my own library. Good stuff is contained in them.

I try to get kids to be a buyer of empty books. Kids find it interesting that I may pay $26 for an empty book. "Why would you do that?" they ask. I pay $26 to press me to see if I can find something worth $26 to write down in that book or journal. All my journals are private, but if you ever read one, you wouldn't have to look very far until you would say, "This is worth more than $26." I must admit, if you glimpsed through my journals, you would say I am a serious student, not just committed to my craft, but committed to life, committed to skills, committed to learning—to see what I can do with seed and soil and sunshine and rain and miracle and possibilities that turn it into life's treasures, family relationships, enterprise sales management, gifts galore, everything I want, all available, especially in America.

I'm asking you to keep a journal. I call a journal one of the three treasures to leave behind.

THREE TREASURES TO LEAVE BEHIND

1. PICTURES

Take a lot of pictures. It's amazing to look back two or three generations at a handful of photographs that tell a story of life in previous times. Wouldn't it be wonderful if you had album after album, thousands of pictures to help tell your story? After all, everyone knows that a picture's worth a thousand words. Don't be lazy in capturing moments. How long does it take to capture an event, an activity? A fraction of a second. How long does it take to miss the event? A fraction of a second. Don't make an error in judgment or discipline. Example: I went to Taipei, Taiwan, for a weekend seminar at the Grand Hotel. There were about 1,000 students in my audience. Guess how many bought their cameras? About 1,000. They all brought their cameras to capture their time at the seminar. They didn't want to miss the event. When you're gone, leave behind the treasure of your life in pictures as well as in words.

2. YOUR LIBRARY

The library is most certainly a treasure. The library you compiled that taught you, instructed you, that helped you defend your ideals and develop a philosophy, the books that inspired you to become wealthy and powerful and healthy and sophisticated and unique. The library that helped you conquer some disease, that helped you to emerge from poverty, that caused you to walk away from the ghetto. The library, the books that fed your mind and fed your soul. Leave your library behind for others to enjoy and learn from. One of the greatest gifts you can leave behind is your library—stepping stones out of the darkness into the light. Your library, your books, leave it all behind for others. Your books will be more valuable than any of the other stuff.

3. YOUR JOURNALS

Your journals contain the ideas that you picked up along life's journey. Wherever you found an occasion to gather something valuable and put it in there so you could go back over it and go back over it until it resonated the wisdom you needed.

Repetition is the mother of skill. Read it one more time. Learn it one more time. See if you can't digest it one more time. Let the ideas coach you again. Let what you recorded teach and inspire you one more time. Words are inspirational, such as the lyrics of a song. If you hear a beautiful song that moves you, you don't say, "Well, that's enough. Don't need to hear that again." No, wouldn't you want to hear it again? And again? Let it instruct you. Let it feed you. Let it teach you. Take you on wings of emotional journeys. Wouldn't you want to do that again? The answer is yes.

Your journals are important. Everything you took the meticulous time to gather is one of the greatest proofs that you are a serious student. Taking pictures, that's pretty easy. Buying a book at a bookstore, that's pretty easy. But it's a little more challenging to be student enough of your own life and your own future and your own destiny. Be student enough to take the time to write the notes and keep the journal. You'll be so glad you did. What a treasure to leave behind when you go. Your journals. Wow. I wouldn't be without mine now.

SEASONS OF LIFE

I'm in Carmel, California, one of my favorite places. It's where I wrote my first book, *Seasons of Life*. I went to this little church one Sunday morning, first time I'd been there, a small church, maybe 150 people. It was a classic sermon that morning— one of the best I've ever heard in all of my life. I happened to have my journal with me this morning. During the sermon, I couldn't believe it was so precise. It was so unique, it was so powerful. Since I had my journal, I'm taking notes of this classic sermon.

Guess how many other people were taking notes? As best I could tell, I was the only one taking notes of this classic sermon. Since I'm a stranger and I'm taking notes, people were looking and most probably thinking, *Who is he and what's he doing?* I started feeling just a little bit uncomfortable, but I continue to write. Now I'm feeling kind of like a spy.

I could hear someone say, "He's going to get out of here with some of this stuff." And I did. I'm the guy who walked away with the good stuff. And because I wrote it all down, I still have the good stuff that I refer to whenever I want to.

I'm asking you to be no less sincere and be no less committed to the advancement of your philosophy. Talk about having your best year ever this year, and then get ready for next year, your very best year ever, and then each year will be the best, year after year. If you commit yourself to some of this simple stuff mentioned in this chapter, you will be amazed at yourself.

Start with a walk around the block. Start with refining your philosophy. Start with your own fabulous mind, where all the answers are, there within the confines of your own mind. Read the books, have personal conversations, listen to sermons, hear the song lyrics, be intrigued by dialogue from a movie. Let your heart be stirred by words. Find ways to capture and incorporate the best of your personal development quest.

All this stuff changed my life. Turned me every way but loose. I've never been the same since my mentor gave me these simple instructions about growth, productivity, and happiness. He taught me:

- How to go from where I was to where I wanted to go.

- How to go from what I was to what I wanted to become.

- How to go from pennies to treasure.
- How to go from nothing to fortune.

You can learn all that too. It's all within the pages of this book that I'm sharing with you, laboring best I can. Words are clumsy at best when trying to describe what's going on in my head, experience, and my heart, but I'm doing my best and I'm excited about it. You're becoming a good student today, and tomorrow, you will see the results of your efforts.

5

YOUR FIVE BEST ABILITIES

I encourage you to develop the five abilities cited in this chapter as part of your personal development quest.

FIVE CRUCIAL ABILITIES: ABSORB, REFLECT, RESPOND, ACT, SHARE

1. DEVELOP THE ABILITY TO ABSORB.

I encourage you to soak up opportunities to improve your life like you're doing right now by reading this book. Be like a sponge. Don't miss anything; I'm not referring to just the words on the page—I mean don't miss the atmosphere, the color, the scenario of what's going on around you every moment. Most people just try to get through each day. But I want you to be committed to learn something new each day. Don't just get through it—get from it. Learn from it. Let

Wherever you are, **be there.**

each day teach you. Join the university of life. What a difference that perspective will make in your future. Commit yourself to learning. Commit yourself to absorbing life as if it's a sponge.

I have a friend who's so gifted in this area. I think he has soaked up and remembers everything that has ever happened to him. He can tell you where he was as a teenager and what he did and what he said, and what she said and how they felt, and the color of the sky and what was going on that day. He gets it. It's actually more exciting to have him tell you about his trip to Acapulco than it is for you to go there yourself. He has an extraordinary gift. No matter where he is, he doesn't miss anything. Here's a good phrase for you to underline and or write in your journal: *Wherever you are, be there.*

Be there to absorb it. Be there to soak it up. Take a picture if you can, and take pictures of your mind. Let your soul and heart take pictures. Get it. Capture it. Absorb it. That's such an important ability to develop—the ability to get it. Don't miss it. Don't be casual in being in the moment. Key phrase: *casualness leads to casualties.*

2. LEARN TO RESPOND.

The ability to respond means let life touch you. Don't let it kill you, but let it touch you. Let sad things make you sad. Let happy things make you happy. Give in to the emotion. Let the emotion strike you. Not just the words, not just the image. Let the feelings strike you. Let the emotions strike you. Here's what's important. Our emotions need to be as educated as our intellect. It's important to know how to feel. It's important to know how to respond. It's important to let life in, let it touch you.

I'm the greatest guy in the world to take to the movies. I get into a good movie. Make me laugh. Make me cry. Scare me to death. Teach me something. Take me high, take me low. Just don't leave me as I was when I came in. Touch my head, heart. Do something to me.

I picked up the newspaper in Australia one time and I saw an advertisement: "See *Doctor Zhivago* on the big screen!" *My gosh, I got to go see it on the big screen,* I thought immediately. I'd seen the movie two or three times before, but not on a big screen. I love the old theaters—the balconies and the chandeliers and the draperies and the big screen. So I went one more time to see *Doctor Zhivago.* And sure enough, I'm swept away again by the story of the Russian Revolution, Doctor Zhivago, and that whole scenario. I had always missed the

83

Our emotions need to be educated as well as our intellect.

importance of the ending of that movie, until this time. The other times I missed it, but this time I got it.

After Comrade General found her, he said, "Tanya, how did you come to be lost?"

And she said, "Well, I was just lost."

He said, "No, how did you come to be lost?"

She said, "Well, the city was on fire when we were running to escape, and I was lost."

He said, "No, how did you come to be lost?" And that's what she didn't want to say. He finally pressed her again, "How did you come to be lost?"

And she said, "Well, while we were running through the city and it was on fire, my father let go of my hand and I was lost." That's what she didn't want to say.

Comrade General said, "Tanya. That's what I've been trying to tell you. Komarovsky was not your real father. He was not. I'm telling you, I've been looking all over for you, and I think I found you. This man, my relative, Dr. Zhivago, the poet, I'm telling you, he was your father."

And Comrade General said, "Tanya, I promise you this, if this man, your real father, had been there, I promise you, he would never have let go of your hand."

And I got it. This time, I got it. The other times, I was eating popcorn, waiting for the movie to finish. Yet, this time I got it. I'm asking you to get it. Absorb life and respond to it.

3. DEVELOP THE ABILITY TO REFLECT.

"Reflect" means go back over, study it again. I encourage you to reflect on your day. Each evening, go back over your day. Who did you see, what did they say, and what happened? How did you feel? What went on? When you reflect, you capture that day. A day is a piece of the mosaic of your life. One: Don't treat your days casually. Two: Get what you can from each day. Three: Reflect; go back over the day, so that it locks into your mind—the experience, the knowledge, sights, sounds, panorama, the color motion picture of the day. Lock it in so that it will serve you in the future, having that day, not missing it.

Also, take a few hours at the end of the week to reflect on the days. Look back over your calendar, your appointment book. Where did you go, who did you see, how did it feel, and what went on? Capture that week in your mind. A week is a pretty good chunk of time.

Next, take half a day at the end of each month, call it your time to reflect, and do the same thing again. Go back over what you read. Go back over what you heard. Go back over what you saw. Go back over the feelings—capture those times to serve you later.

And then, set aside a weekend at the end of the year to establish that year firmly in your consciousness, firmly in your experience bank, so that you have it, so that it never disappears.

This is a good ability to develop, the ability to reflect, review. Remember, remember, remember. It's so valuable to be able to remember the thought, remember the idea, remember the experience, remember the occasion, remember the day, remember the weather, remember the emotion, remember the complexity, remember the highs, remember the lows. So valuable at the end of the day. Lock in that day. Lock in that week. Lock in that month. Lock in the year. Journaling will help with this ability to reflect and remember.

There's also something to be said for solitude when you reflect. Sometimes you can reflect with somebody. A husband and wife reflect on the past year. Parents reflect with their children on the past year. How did we do it? And how didn't we do it? And how could we improve? Colleagues can reflect with each other. But you also have to learn to reflect with yourself. There's something to be said for solitude, for taking occasions to shut out the world and everything else for a while.

How do I reflect in solitude? I have a motor home; and with my motorcycle on the back of it, I head for the mountains and ride the Jeep trails. There are very few human beings on the Jeep trails. Or I travel out into the desert somewhere. This is my time to get away. I live a very public life, so I treasure solitude, a chance to reflect alone, to go back over my life, to go

It's important to reflect to make the past more valuable, to serve you for the future.

back over my skills, my experiences. Alone. There are some things you need to do alone. Ponder, think, wonder, read, study, absorb, soak in. Try to become better at reflecting this year than you were last year. Seek solitude.

An even closer way to get alone to reflect is to go to a closet (bedroom, study, den, bathroom, wherever) for time of meditation, time of prayer. When you go into your space, close the door. Shut out everything other than what you want to reflect upon. Life is so full of experiences: touching, seeing, looking, doing, acting, speaking, listening, disciplines, and on and on. But sometimes, we need to shut the door and just wonder, pray, contemplate, think, and let things move into our consciousness and awareness that can be done no other way.

While flying down the freeway, it's difficult to get through to what we need to think about, pray about. So many things to do, it's difficult to get through to a time of reflection. But times of solitude, times to reflect are so valuable. Learn to reflect. It's important to reflect to make the past more valuable, to serve you for the future.

What's really powerful is learning to gather up the past and invest it in the future. Gather up today and invest it in tomorrow. Gather up this week and invest it in the next week. Gather up this year and invest it in the next year. That truth is so powerful. Rather than just hanging on one more year, hanging in there, seeing what's going to happen—learn, study reflect, act.

This is part of the personal development quest, becoming better than you are, more valuable than you are, not just in terms of economics—also in terms of motherhood, fatherhood, being a better brother, better colleague, making a better contribution to the family, to society, to the community, to the church, to the office, to the commitment, to the partnership.

Work on yourself. Then you bring more value to the partnership, to the marriage, to the franchise, the corporation, enterprise, community, and to the nation. The best contribution you can make to someone else is self-development. Not self-sacrifice. Self-sacrifice only earns contempt. Self-development earns respect. Pity the mother who says, "I'm going to give up my life for my children."

Self-sacrifice is not noble. Self-investment is noble, from self-development. If I work on myself and become more valuable, think of what that does for friendship. I used to use the old expression, "You take care of me and I'll take care of you." But I found out how shallow and short-ended that statement was, and I changed it to this: "I'll take care of me for you, if you

Gather up the past and **invest it in the future.**

will please take care of you for me." And this is part of personal development, that we work harder on ourselves than we do on our job, to the benefit of us and others.

Now we bring that attitude to friendship. Now we bring that to our marriage. Now we bring that to our family relationships as a father or mother, and we develop the strength and power we need to excel in all areas. This scenario of disciplines and the abilities to acquire those gifts and skills add to our value, so we bring more to each experience. Now, we bring more to the next week, the next month, the next year. If you follow this discipline—absorb, respond, and reflect—your life will take on more meaning for yourself and others.

I said to my father when he was about to turn 76 years old, "Dear father of mine, can you imagine what it's going to be like to gather up the last 75 years of your life and invest them in your 76th year?" What a difference of philosophy—rather than just hanging on one more year. Gather up 75 and invest them in the next one. Gather up the last six years and invest them in the next year. That's powerful communication. So powerful.

So consider this: One, the ability to absorb. Second, the ability to respond. Third, the ability to reflect.

4. DEVELOP THE ABILITY TO ACT.

Take action. Not hasty if it isn't required, but don't lose much time to act. The time to act is when the idea is hot and the emotion is strong. You say, "Mr. Rohn, I'd like to have a library like yours." My response, "If you feel strongly about that step, go get your first book, and then get the second book. Go before the feeling passes and before the idea gets dim. Take action pronto, immediately. Take action as soon as possible."

If you don't take action right away, we call what happens the "law of diminishing intent." We intend to take action when the idea strikes us; we intend to act when the emotion is high. But if you don't translate that into action quickly, the intent starts to diminish, diminish, diminish. And a month from now, the idea is cold. A year from now, it can't be found. So act as soon as possible on each idea. Set up a discipline. When emotions are high and the idea is strong and clear and powerful, that's the time to set up the discipline to act, to follow through and take the next step.

If someone talks about good health and you're stirred, say, "I need to get a book on nutrition and read it." Get the book before the idea passes and before the emotion gets cold. Go

Everything matters.

for the book, start the library, start the process, fall on the floor, do some pushups. Action. You must take action. Otherwise, the wisdom is wasted. Otherwise, the emotion soon passes—unless you put it into a disciplined activity. Capture it. Discipline is how to capture the emotion and wisdom and translate it into reality.

What's important about disciplines? All disciplines affect each other. In fact, here's a good philosophical phrase: *Everything affects everything else. Nothing stands alone.* Don't be naive in saying, "Well, this doesn't matter." I'm telling you, everything matters. There are some things that matter more than others, but there isn't anything that doesn't matter. Every letdown affects the rest of your performance. This is an important part of the educational process when working on personal development.

If you don't take the walk around the block, you probably won't eat an apple a day. If you don't eat the apple a day, you probably won't build your library. If you don't build your library, you probably won't keep a journal, and you won't take pictures, then you won't do wise things with your money, won't do wise things with your time, won't do wise things with your possibilities and relationships. And the first thing you know, six years have accumulated, and you realize that you have messed up. So the whole key to reversing that process now is to start picking up these disciplines: exercising, healthy eating, learning, etc.

Now, here's the positive side. Every new and beneficial discipline affects the rest of your disciplines. Every new one affects the rest. That's why action is so important. Even the least and smallest action matters, so take it. When you start seeing accomplishments and your value returns from that one action, you will be inspired to do the next one, and the next one, and the next one.

When you start walking around the block, you will be inspired to eat an apple. Eat an apple, and you will be inspired to get a book. Read a book, and you will be inspired to get a journal. Write in a journal, and you will be inspired to grow, develop some skills, and be productive. All disciplines affect each other, and they all lead to a happy lifestyle. Every lack affects the rest. Every new affects the rest. The key is to diminish the lack and set up the new—then you've started a whole new life process.

Also, one more thought on discipline. The greatest value of discipline is self-worth, self-esteem. Others teach self-esteem these days, but they don't connect it to disciplines. I believe that the least lack of discipline starts to erode our

The greatest value of discipline is self-worth, self-esteem.

philosophy, our standards, and even our ethics. One of the greatest temptations is to just ease up a little bit regarding your values, integrity, and honesty. But even the slightest lack of doing your best will erode your standards. Instead of doing your best, doing just a little less than your best may seem to be okay.

You tell yourself, "Well, it won't hurt to just slack off a little. It will only affect my sale a little." No, it's going to affect your consciousness. It's going to affect your philosophy. Now you've begun to affect your own philosophy, and not in a good way. The problem with the least neglect, not doing your best, is that it acts like an infection. If you don't get rid of it, it becomes a disease; and one neglect leads to another.

If you find yourself in a diseased state, and your self-worth, self-confidence, and self-value have diminished, all you have to do to get back on track is start the smallest discipline that corresponds to your philosophy, like I should, and I could, and I will. Say, "No longer will I let neglect stack up on me so that I will have the sorry scenario six years from now, giving some excuse instead of celebrating my progress." Start walking around the block again, eating that apple again, whatever you need to do to do your best.

Let's get kids involved in the least of disciplines. Adding one more, and then one more, and then another one, and soon you are weaving the tapestry of a disciplined life into which you can pour more wisdom, more positive attitude, more strength, more faith, and more courage. Now these kids have something they can build upon.

And when you do the same for yourself, the success and growth and productivity and joy will flow. The early return will have you so excited that you'll commit yourself to this strategy

Take advantage of every opportunity, no matter how small it seems.

for the rest of your life. You'll never go back to the old ways. Join a new crowd. Join a new group. You have the disciplines to do it. To take action to live your best life ever.

Previously in this book, I recommended reading *The Richest Man in Babylon*. I've lectured now to more than three million people in the past 33 years, and I've recommended this little book to almost all of them. Guess how many actually got this little book and read it. Answer? Very few. My best guess is 10 percent. Yet it is such good advice: Number one, it's easy to find. Number two, it's easy to buy. And number three, it's easy to read. It's in story form. That's why I use it for teenagers. So if it's easy to find, easy to buy, and easy to read, why wouldn't everybody want to follow my advice? You don't know. I don't know. Nobody knows. So about 10 percent do and about 90 percent don't or won't. That's a mystery.

But I'm telling you, 10 years from now, those numbers will still be the same. The numbers don't change, only the faces change. I used to belong to the 90 percent who couldn't be bothered, even if it was easy.

Do you have a library card? Libraries make the wisdom of the world available; you can transform your life in any value amount you want by taking advantage of reading books that are free to borrow. It is possible to transform your life spiritually, socially, personally, economically, and every other way. You can learn how to be rich, powerful, sophisticated, healthy, and influential. You don't need a good luck charm or rabbit's foot. You don't need multitrack affirmations. Affirmation without discipline is the beginning of delusion.

Don't let anyone sweep you into some contrary way to nature itself. Nature says you must labor to receive the harvest

Affirmation without discipline is the beginning of delusion.

after the miracle of the seed, the soil, the seasons, sunshine, rain, and God. It is only available to you by labor, so labor well. Learn well. Discipline yourself well, and you can have all the treasures you want. You don't have to move to Sedona, where all the force fields come together in Arizona. No.

Let's teach our kids the simple ways to transform their health, number one. Their economics, number two. Their ability to communicate, number three. Their life, treasure, and lifestyle, number four. Spirituality, number five. And the list goes on and on. Let's not leave out any of the least of disciplines that encourages the next one, to do the next one, to do the next one.

First thing you know, this whole beautiful life scenario is spinning up toward you. It's as simple as starting, committing yourself to life change. And once you begin this journey down this road, I promise that you will reap a great harvest season after season.

We're going to talk financial independence in just a little while, but right now, guess how many people can retire from the income of their own personal resources when it comes time to retire? Answer? About 5 percent. In the most independent country in the world, 95 percent are dependent, and 5 percent are independent. Take charge of your own retirement. If you take charge of your own retirement through personal development and all the skills you've been reading about, (plus financial independence coming up in another chapter), you can *multiply* it at least by 5, maybe by 10, maybe by 20, maybe by 100. On the other hand, if you allow the government or some company to take care of it, you will have to *divide* by 5.

Take charge!

Take charge of your own life. Take charge of your own day. Take charge of your own conversation. Take charge of your own family. Take charge of your own possibilities. Learn these skills, develop these kinds of strategies, and life will open up for you.

Don't talk like people who blame others for their station in life. Lend a helping hand, but don't fall into their poor philosophical scenario. Don't blame what they blame. Don't use the excuses they use. It's called the language of the poor. Switch gears, switch language, switch ideas, switch strategy. Start with the simplest of disciplines. And don't demean any of these disciplines. The smallest of disciplines starts the process of life change. And if you invest in discipline, you can have whatever you wish. It's called the beginning of a miracle.

Develop these strengths abilities: absorb; respond; reflect; act; share.

5. DEVELOP THE ABILITY TO SHARE.

Develop the ability to pass along to someone else what has already benefited you. If you've picked up a good idea today while reading this book, pass it along. Don't let it whither on the vine. Pass it along. If you read a good book, pass it along. Say, "Hey, I read a book that really helped me—it got me thinking." Or, "I read a book that helped me improve my health." "I read a book that inspired me." Pass it along, share with others your good fortune.

Here's what is exciting about sharing. If you share with ten different people, they get to hear it once—and you get to hear it again ten times. So it's probably going to do more for you than it is for them. And as they say, "Everybody wins." When you share, everybody wins.

Share your ideas. Share your experiences. Share your knowledge. You can have just as much pleasure as I do. I say that presenting seminars is one of my joys in life. I make the best investment I can of words, spirit, heart, soul, time, and energy.

At this stage in my life, I don't have to work this hard—traveling, giving seminars, writing books—but I gladly work this hard. Why? I want the return. I want to hear people say, "Your words touched my life." See, that's heavyweight stuff. You can't buy it with money. It makes me happy to know I'm making a difference in people's lives.

You can get the same reward by recommending a book. Somebody will read that book, and then they'll read another one, and they'll read another one, and they'll come to you someday and say, "You got me started. That book you recommended turned my lights on, turned my mind around, got me thinking, got me pondering, and I've been on track ever since." You can get just as much praise as I do if you share—share with your children, share with your colleagues, share with everybody who comes within your grasp.

Sharing not only helps you, it helps the person you share with. Here's what else sharing does—it makes you bigger than you are. If I have a full glass of water, can that glass hold any more water if it's full? The answer is yes. But for it to hold more, you have to pour out what's already in the glass. That's what I'm asking you to do. If you're full of ideas, if you're full of good things, I'm asking you to pour it out. Why? Because more will be poured in.

When you do pour out, you become bigger because human beings have the ability to grow in consciousness and awareness and capacity. Capacity is unlimited.

For example, in Europe, many kids speak two or three languages. When I grew up, my father spoke German, but he never taught me. My mother spoke French, but she never taught me. They were trying to get away from the "old world" languages back then. They had no concept of how valuable languages were going to be in the future, so they abandoned the German, abandoned the French. I could have learned all three languages instead of just English.

My girls attended school in Beverly Hills, where they offered three languages for the students to learn: French, German, and Spanish. Why? Because kids can learn two languages just as easy as one. How many languages can a child learn? As many as you take the time to teach them. They do not lack capacity. They only lack teachers. Wow.

Expand your capacity by sharing what you have, **your experiences,** what you've learned.

And the same is true for you. You don't lack capacity—and you expand your capacity by sharing what you have, what you've experienced, what you've learned.

I'm still working for a very self-interest reason. If I share with you, my consciousness grows. If I share with you, I get to hear all this good stuff again. Somebody asked me not long ago, "Mr. Rohn, how are you doing in life? You get on everybody's case pretty hard during the seminars. How are *you* doing with all this stuff you teach?"

I said, "The best answer to that I can share with you is this: Listen to me very carefully, but don't watch me too closely. This stuff of life easier to lecture on than it is to do. I understand that. I'm working on it, just like you. But I can attest to the fact that your capacity grows the more you learn."

Why should you want your capacity to grow? To hold more of the next experience. So am I saying some people will get more out of sitting in a seminar audience or reading a book than others will get? The answer is yes. If you haven't been into expanding your own capacity lately, you might not get much from a seminar or book. But if you've been into expanding your capacity and you've been sharing and you've been doing all this best-life stuff, there's no limit to what all this could mean to you today and in the future. This is your chance to grow, change, develop, absorb, and take in every opportunity.

I'm asking you to expand and grow so you can hold more of the next experience. Some people aren't very happy. Happiness could be poured out on the whole world, yet some people just can't be happy. Why? They're not big enough. Those who are small don't get much out of life. Those who are small in comprehension, small in the ability to think and wonder, small in appreciation. No matter how much happiness and good things are poured out, they don't grasp it.

Prosperity can be poured out on the whole country, yet some people are not very prosperous. Why? They're too small in their thinking, too small in their ability to share, and they have not expanded to their full capacity. Don't be like that.

Learn to share. It's a glorious, glorious experience.

6

GOAL-SETTING STRATEGIES

Now let's talk about goal-setting strategies. Let's learn how to set goals. Not long after I met Mr. Shoaff, we were having breakfast one morning. Mr. Shoaff said, "Mr. Rohn, now that we're acquainted and we know each other fairly well, maybe one of the best ways I can help you is if you let me see your current list of goals. Let's go over them and talk about it."

I said, "What? I don't have a list of goals."

He said, "Well, Mr. Rohn, if you don't have a list of your goals, I can guess your bank balance within a few hundred dollars." Which he did, and that got my attention.

I said, "You mean my bank balance would change if I had a list of goals?"

He said, "Drastically."

So that day, I became a student of setting goals and I've used it to dynamically affect my life. I've taught it to some of my business colleagues. We use it to do business around the world. Setting goals is a very important aspect of living your best year ever—setting goals for growth, increased productivity, and enjoying a happy life.

YOUR VISION OF THE FUTURE

Goals are your vision of the future. There are two ways to face the future: One, with apprehension. Two, with anticipation. Guess how most people face the future? With apprehension. Why? The major reason is because they don't have their future well-designed. They allowed their future to be designed by someone else.

If you don't make plans for your own future, guess what? You will most likely fall into someone else's plans. And guess what someone else may have planned for you? "Not much."

Goals are your vision of the future.

Your own ability to design your own future **counts very much!**

You must make a list of your goals, what you want your future to be.

All their lives, too many people count on this "not much" list. If all of your relatives with negative attitudes suddenly turn positive, what will that do for your future? Not much. If prices come down a little, what will that do for your future? Not much. If the economy gets a little better, what will that do for your future? Not much. If circumstances get a little better, what will that do? Not much. If the weather gets a little better over the next few years, that will do not much.

You could list many more "not much" scenarios that most people count on all their lives with their fingers crossed. That's why ten years from now, they will be driving a vehicle they don't want to drive, living where they don't want to live, wearing what they don't want to wear, doing what they don't want to do, having what they don't want to have, and maybe become what they didn't want to become. And it all starts by counting on something that counts "not much."

THE PROMISE OF THE FUTURE

How can your life change dramatically? You must count on yourself—especially on your own ability to design your own future. It's called the promise of the future; and if you design it well with inspired appreciation, it will have a positively awesome effect on your life.

But if you face the future with apprehension, you will take hesitant steps all day, uncertain steps all day. And if you take uncertain steps all day for six years, you can imagine how empty your life can be.

Connected to the promise is the price—the price to pay for an exciting future. The price is easy if the promise is clear and powerful. But the price will seem almost too much to pay, too much to get over, too much to accomplish if the promise isn't clear, if the promise isn't powerful.

Even young people will pay the disciplines if they can see the promise. One of our biggest challenges as parents is to help our kids see the promise of the future. That's why I teach financial independence, how to become wealthy, powerful, sophisticated, healthy, and unique. All of what kids hope for is possible in the United States of America. That's the promise of the future. The price? A few simple disciplines practiced every day. Youths will pay the price of the simple disciplines if they can see the promise of the future. But if they can't see it, they don't want to pay.

The price is easy if the promise is clear and powerful.

And the same is true of all of us. We will pay the most extraordinary disciplines if we can see the promise of the future. This is called setting goals. So I'm asking you to get a handle on the future. I'm asking you not to leave it to anyone else. Don't leave it to the company. Companies have their own goals. I'm asking you to set your own goals, your personal goals, income goals, financial goals, health goals, and spiritual goals. Where do you want to go, what do you want to do, what do you want to see, and what do you want to be. That's it—write your own promise of the future. Design your own future. It's within your hands and your capacity to do so.

Here's how simple a goal-setting strategy is. It's not mysterious. You don't have to anchor. You don't have to focus. You don't have to visualize. None of that. Here's how simple goal setting is—decide what you want and write it down. That's how profound this strategy is.

Decide what you want and write it down. Make a list. Suggestions include:

- Where do you want to go?
- What do you want to do?
- What do you want to see?
- What do you want to be?
- What do you want to have?
- What do you want to share?
- What projects would you like to support?
- What would you like to be known for?
- What skills would you like to learn?
- What are some extraordinary things you'd like to do?
- What ordinary, simple things would you like to do?

Decide what you want **and write it down.**

- What silly little things would you like to do?

- What are some very important things you'd like to do?

Decide and write it all down. And if this is your own private list, put some of it in code that nobody else can understand if it fell into unfriendly hands. Write down whatever foolish things come to mind, it doesn't matter. It's your list.

I actually had a little revenge on my first list. There was a finance company who used to harass me. I was two or three payments behind, and this one guy called incessantly saying, "We're going to come get your car, drag it rear end up down the street in front of your neighbors." He put me down something fierce. When I met Earl Shoaff and straightened out my life, one of the first things on one of my lists was that finance company guy.

At the time, I needed a little drama in my life, so when I finally got the money to pay them off, I put it in small bills in a big briefcase and walked into the office on Wilshire Boulevard in Los Angeles. I walked to the guy's office who harassed me so often. I opened the door, walked in, right up to his desk, stood right in front of him, looked him straight in the eye, not saying a word.

He said, "Well, what are you doing here?"

I opened the briefcase, dumped the pile of money all over his desk, and said, "Count it. It's all there. I'll never be back." Then I turned around, walked out, and slammed the door behind me. Now that might not be noble, but just try it at least one time. Pay off with a little drama. Then I checked that off my goals list.

Keep your list with you. I keep my list in my journal so I can go back and review it. I can look at the list I made five years ago. I'm a little embarrassed when I look at past lists and see what I thought was so important. Oh, how my philosophy has changed from ten years ago, five years ago, three years ago. What's valuable to me now is different from what it was then. Keep all of your lists of goals—each shows your growth, your ability to change, and reveals how your philosophy has expanded and your values and disciplines.

My Japanese friend, Toro Ikeda, put on his first goals list to hire a Caucasian gardener. I thought that was good. I liked that. Do you realize just how profound setting goals is?

In addition to your personal private list, you may want to get together with your wife and make a list. Get together with your kids, decide, and make a list. Get together with your

Setting goals is an important part of your future.

business colleagues, decide, and make a list. That's how easy it is.

Here's one more scenario on setting goals. When I started making my first list, Mr. Shoaff said, "Mr. Rohn, looks like we're going to be together for a while. I have a suggestion for you. You're a 25-year-old American male. Sure, you've made some mistakes, but now you're on the road to better things. You have a family, so you have every reason to think about my suggestion. Among all the goals you're going to set, why don't you set a goal to become a millionaire? This is America and all the possibilities are available. Why don't you set a goal to become a millionaire? It's got a nice ring to it, and enough zeros to impress your accountant."

And then he said, "Here's why."

Now, I thought, The man doesn't need to teach me why. It would be great to have a million dollars!

As if he read my mind, he said, "No, that's not it. Here's why."

Then he shared one of the greatest lessons I ever learned— and I'm about to share it with you. This wisdom is worth the price of reading this book if you can capture what I'm about to share with you. You may have missed your favorite television show to read this book. But what I'm about to share with you changed my whole life.

Mr. Shoaff said, "Set a goal to become a millionaire—for what it will make of you to achieve it."

That was one of the greatest lessons in one sentence that I've ever received in my life. Set a goal that will make you stretch—for what it will make of you to achieve it. What a brand-new reason for setting goals. What an all-encompass-ing challenge to have a better vision of the future, to see what

The greatest value in life is not what you get—it's what you become.

it will make of you to achieve it. And here's why: The greatest value in life is not what you get. The greatest value in life is what you become.

The question to ask on the job is not, "What am I getting here?" The best question to ask is, "What am I becoming here?" It's not what you get that makes you valuable—it's what you become that makes you valuable.

So Mr. Shoaff said, "Set a goal to become a millionaire for what it'll make of you to achieve it." Then he said, "When you finally become a millionaire, what's important is not the money."

I thought, Wow, I've got some more to learn.

"I was rich by the time I was 31. I was a millionaire—but I was broke by the time I was 33. I didn't give it all away, I lost it all. I made foolish mistakes. I was a farm boy from Idaho. That early money drove me bonkers. I used to say of something I wanted, "How many colors does it come in? I'll buy them all." I just went crazy over that first money. And then I made that one foolish mistake. I didn't understand the bank's "continuing guarantee" policy. I was so naive coming off the farm that I didn't know what continuing means.

That and a few other mistakes, and by the time I was 33, I was broke. I made and lost millions since then, but what an experience that was. And I'm telling you, the man was right. When I was broke at age 33, guess what I discovered? The money did not mean that much. It represented only a fraction of all my assets.

Mr. Shoaff was right: "Once you become a millionaire, Mr. Rohn, you could give all the money away, because you will discover that what's important is not the money. What's important is the person you've become."

Set the kind of goals that will make something of you to achieve them.

Now let me give you the key phrase on setting goals: Set the kind of goals that will make something of you to achieve them. Always keep that in mind. *What will reaching this goal make of me? If I set this goal and go for it, not only will I achieve it, but what will it make of me in the process?* This was a whole new concept I learned about setting goals. I share this with you as wisdom learned and earned during the process.

TWO PARTS TO GOAL SETTING FOR WHAT YOU BECOME

There are two parts to goal setting for what you become: 1) Don't set your goals too low, and 2) Don't compromise or sell out. Let's look at both in depth.

Number one: Don't set your goals too low. We teach this in leadership classes, too. Don't join an easy crowd. You won't grow. Go where the expectations are high. Go where the demands are challenging. Go where the pressure is on to perform, to grow, to change, to develop, to read, to study, to develop skills.

I belong to a small group, and we do business around the world. You cannot believe the expectations at that level, what we expect of each other in terms of excellence. Far beyond average. Why? So we can each grow, so that we can receive from the group, we can contribute to the group something unprecedented. It's called living at the summit.

Go where the demands are high. Go where the expectations are strong, so you will be provoked, you will be pushed. Refuse to remain the same for the next couple of years, the next five years— insist instead that you'll grow and change.

Don't set your goals too low. The person who says, "Well, I don't need much," will most likely not become much.

Number two: Don't compromise. Don't sell out. There were some things I went for back in the early years that I paid too big a price for. If I'd known how much it was going to cost me, I never would've paid. But I didn't know. So don't sell out. An ancient phrase says, "Count the cost." And an ancient story says, "Judas got the money." You say, "Well, that's a success story." No, no. It's true that 30 pieces of silver in those days was a sizeable fortune, but Judas was a traitor. He condemned an innocent Man. And after he had the money in his hot little hands, he was so unhappy that he committed suicide.

Somebody asks, "Well, if you had a fortune, how could you be unhappy?" He wasn't unhappy with the money. He was unhappy with himself. The greatest source of unhappiness is

The ultimate source of unhappiness **is self-unhappiness.**

self-unhappiness. The greatest source of unhappiness doesn't come from outside. The most powerful source of unhappiness comes from inside.

And inside is where erosion starts, doing a little less than you could. That's where the beginning infection of unhappiness starts, doing a little less than you can, not feeling good about yourself. Don't let that happen.

Judas was unhappy, so he tried to give back the money. They threw him out with his money. Then he decided to just throw away the money. Which he did. After his fortune was gone, he realized he couldn't change what he had become, a traitor. So he hung himself. Why such a tragic end? Because he was so unhappy with himself. He sold out for money.

Ancient script sums it all up, *"And what do you benefit if you gain the whole world but lose your own soul? Is anything worth more than your soul?"*[1] Don't sell out. Don't compromise your values. Don't compromise your virtues. Don't compromise your philosophy.

BEHOLD AND BEWARE

Here are two key words: behold and beware—both are necessary to understand in our context of setting goals. *Behold* is a positive word. I strongly urge you to behold the possibilities, behold the opportunity, behold the drama, behold the awesomeness, behold the uniqueness, behold the majesty in your life. Behold daily, even moment by moment. *Beware* is a negative word. Beware of the temptation to sell out. Beware of what you become in pursuit of what you want. Beware of negative results. Beware of the kind of goals you set, ensuring they lead to a positive and successful future.

Always set goals that will transform your life, make you far better than you are, far stronger than you are. Good advice. Remember it.

HAPPINESS

During that same conversation, Mr. Shoaff said, "Mr. Rohn, if you wish to be happy, study happiness." I didn't know happiness was a study. My best hope for happiness at age 25 was to just go through the day with my fingers crossed, hoping- somehow, something would make me happy.

He said, "No, Mr. Rohn. Happiness is not something you postpone. Happiness is not something off in the future. Happiness is something you design."

Happiness is something you study and then design.

Happiness is a practice. Happiness is an art. It's not an accident. It's an art, and anyone who wants to be happy can study and practice the art. Happy living and a happy lifestyle is a culture you can make happen. Money doesn't make you cultured, but culture is within the grasp of all of us.

How much does a book cost that teaches sophistication, refinement, sensibility, and civility? $4,000? No—$40. I'm telling you, in America, everything's available. Everything's within reach. All you have to be is committed to it and study it. Culture is a study. Civility is a study. It's not an amount. It's not an account. It's a study. Money doesn't make you sophisticated and cultured. I know a guy who is rich, yet he's a clod. He eats with his elbow in his soup. He's crass and rude. There is nothing much more pitiful than a rich clod. It's a sad thing to see. Money doesn't make you respectable. Only study and practice make you civil in a civil society. Only study and practice make you cultured and only study and practice make you happy.

Study and practice make you rich, so don't be lazy in learning. First, study and practice how to do well. Next, study and practice how to live well. Don't be lazy in learning and practicing the arts of economics, productivity, and a lifestyle of joy.

Earl Shoaff taught me in such simple but extraordinary terms. "Mr. Rohn, suppose you're getting your shoes shined. When he's finished, you see he has done an exceptional job. In fact you just got one of the world's all-time great shines. When you pay him, you realize you have some extra change. A question pops into your mind, *Should I give him one quarter or two quarters as a tip for my neat shine?*" Here's what Shoaff said. "If two amounts pop in your mind, always

Study and practice **makes you respectable, cultured, and rich.**

go for the higher amount and become the higher thinking person." That helped change my life. He said, "Become a two-quarter person."

Now you can tell that was a long time ago when a quarter was a good tip. Now it takes dollars, so just substitute dollars for quarters.

Then Mr. Shoaff told me, "If you're wondering if you should give the guy one quarter or two quarters and you decide to give him just one quarter, that decision will affect you the rest of the day. Every time you look down and see that great shine on your shoes, you'll think, *I'm really cheap. One lousy quarter tip for a great shine that will last for days.*

"But," Mr. Shoaff continued, "When you go for giving the two quarters, you won't believe the extra happiness you can buy for just an extra quarter."

That's called studying and practicing the art of a positive lifestyle, which means living well.

A father wads up a $20 bill, throws it at his son, and says, "If you need the darn stuff that bad, take it. Just get out of my face." How sad. A father with money and no joy; he studied economics, but he never studied joy. I'm asking you to turn around that type of thinking. Turn that all around from negative to positive, from sadness to joyfulness.

I gave a seminar in Saint Louis, Missouri, and when I finished it, a man walked up and said, "Mr. Rohn, you've really gotten to me. I'm going to change my philosophy. I'm going to change my attitude. I'm going to change my life. I'm going to change everything. You've touched me today, and you'll hear about me. You'll hear my story someday."

I said, "Okay." A lot of people say things. Sure enough, though, a few months later, I went back to Saint Louis to present another seminar. When I finished, this man came walking up to me. I didn't remember his name, but he said, "I'm sure you'll remember me as the man who said, 'I'm going to go make some changes. You've touched me today.'"

I said, "I do remember you."

He said, "I'm telling you, things are already happening for me. I can't believe it, and in just a matter of months. One of the things I decided to change was my relationship with my family. My wife and I have two lovely teenage daughters. Parents couldn't ask for any more beautiful, lovely daughters. I'm the only one who has given them trouble. These daughters of ours have never given us any trouble, yet I've usually been the one all these years who gave them all the trouble."

He continued, "My daughters love to go to rock concerts, and I'm always giving them trouble. They have to beg me for the money. I tell them, 'I don't want you to go. You stay out too late. The music's too loud. You're going to ruin your hearing. You won't be able to hear the rest of your life.' I just get on their case. But they keep begging, keep begging. Finally, when they beg long enough, I say, 'All right, here's the money. If you have to go that bad, just go.' That's how I've been up until now."

But then he said, "After I left your seminar, I decided to change all that to what you taught as a positive lifestyle of living. And you won't believe it. Not long ago, I saw that one of their favorite performers was coming to town. Guess what I did? I went down and bought the tickets myself. I brought them home, put them in an envelope, and when I saw my daughters later that day, I handed them the envelope, I said to my two lovely daughters, 'You may not believe it, but inside this envelope are two tickets for the upcoming concert.' They couldn't believe it. 'And you'll be happy to know that your begging days are over.'" They were speechless.

He said, "Next I told them, 'Now don't open the envelope until you get to the concert.'"

They said okay "So they go to the concert, open the envelope, and hand the tickets to the usher. He says, 'Follow me,' and he starts walking toward the front. The girls say, 'Hey, hold it. Hold it. Something must be wrong.' The usher takes another look and says, 'No, nothing's wrong. Follow me.'

"He motions them into the 10th row, center. The only tickets they were ever able to beg for was right, third balcony, where they could hardly see the stage. I stayed up a little late that night. Sure enough, a little after midnight, my two daughters come bursting through the front door. One of them lands in my lap. The other one has her arms around my neck. They're both saying, 'You're one of the all-time world's greatest fathers!'"

He said, "Mr. Rohn, you're right. I can't believe it—same money, different father. I've started making the changes, and I decided to start with my teenagers, my girls. And what a difference it's making in my life."

You can do that with your lifestyle. You can do it with your sales career. You can do it with your management career. You can do it with any part of your life. If you're looking for the best in your life, happiness unmatched, do not curse the only thing you really have—seed and soil, sunshine, rain, miracles, and seasons. Start changing and processing and evaluating and recovering today what you've been lacking—and this process of change will work for you. You will not believe what can happen in such a short period of time.

NOTE

1. Matthew 16:26 NLT.

7

FINANCIAL INDEPENDENCE

L et's now delve into the topic of financial independence. Everybody has to wrestle with their own concept of financial independence, getting rich, or becoming wealthy. Some people are a little uncomfortable with those kinds of phrases, and I can understand that. We've heard the phrase, which is true, that the love of money can certainly be evil. But money itself isn't evil. There are some evil ways to acquire it. And there is a difference between greed and ambition.

Contrary to the 1987 movie *Wall Street,* greed is not good. Greed is evil and must be dealt with. Greed hopes for something for nothing. Greed hopes for more than its share. Greed hopes for something at the expense of others. We call that evil. And people who are greedy and take unfair advantage of others should be locked up. Make them pay the price of being selfish. Greed is not good.

What is good? Ambition, legitimate ambition. Legitimate ambition says I only want something at the *service* of others, not the expense of others. Good is using our financial resources for the betterment of our family and others—meeting the needs of ourselves and others, devoted to one another.

Jesus gave the greatest scenario for success when He said, "No one can serve two masters. For you will hate one and love the other; you will be devoted to one and despise the other. You cannot serve God and be enslaved to money."[1]

Greed causes the calamity of many. The greed for power and wealth caused Stalin in his day and time to kill 30 million of his own countryfolk. His greed and lust for power was catastrophic. The well-known statement is true—absolute power corrupts absolutely. Stalin sought power at the expense of others, not at the service of others.

But Jesus turns the whole scenario around and says that service to many leads to great wealth. Service to many leads to great recognition. Service to many leads to great satisfaction. Zig Ziglar frequently said, "If you help enough people get what they want, you can have everything you want." That's not greed. It's called legitimate ambition at the service of others.

But I know some people struggle with this idea of wanting more. Some people are a bit disturbed knowing that I've been teaching kids all these years how to be rich by age 40, by 35 if they're extra bright, and even sooner if they find a unique opportunity. Some don't agree with me about teaching young people how to make a fortune.

So, over the years, I've modified the wording a little bit—now I set their goal to become "financially independent." This term is a little softer than wanting to be rich and make a fortune; it's easier to comprehend without seeming brazen or arrogant.

Financial independence: the ability to live from the income of your own personal resources.

My definition of financial independence is the ability to live from the income of your own personal resources. I think financial independence is a powerful and worthy goal. I think it is a legitimate ambition to render good service, to develop skills in the marketplace, and to become so valuable that you can have resources, and then eventually have enough resources that are so well-invested that you can live independent from the income of your own personal resources.

If you make wise decisions with your resources and income, you will be able to do all the things you'd like to do, the projects you'd like to support, things you'd like to take care of that you can't take care of now. I think being financially independent is a worthy ambition.

A FINANCIAL STATEMENT

Now let's talk about financial independence. Mr. Shoaff said, "Mr. Rohn, first of all, we need to take a picture of where you are. To get where you want to go, you have to take a picture of where you are now. One of the best ways to take a financial picture of where you are now is to create a financial statement, which will reveal any mistakes in the past that we can correct into disciplines for the future."

I wasn't sure what a financial statement was, so he taught me. Mr. Shoaff said, "It's this simple. On a sheet of paper, list the value of all your assets on this side, and then add each and put the total at the bottom of the list. Then, on the other side, list everything you owe, which are called your liabilities, add up the value of that, and put the total at the bottom of the list.

A financial statement reveals your current economic situation.

Then you subtract one from the other and you come up with your current net worth."

He continued. "This total is not your total net worth—because it doesn't include what you're worth as a parent, a spouse, a business colleague, and a human being. That's not part of this calculation. On a financial statement, we look at economics. And if you're messed up here, you might be messed up elsewhere in your life. You might come up short in some other areas."

It's so important not to be short in faith, in language, not to be short in capacity. It's so important not to be short in spirit, in personal development, not to be short in uniqueness. So sure, there are a lot more values here than just economics. But the reason we take a picture of economics is to illustrate that part of your life.

Mr. Shoaff said, "Mr. Rohn, if you haven't done wise things with your money, you probably haven't done wise things with your time, and you haven't done wise things with your friendships, you haven't done wise things with your family relationships. One mistake leads to another."

So he said, "First of all, you must straighten out your finances, so let's take a picture."

I said, "Well, if I put this financial statement together, mine wouldn't look that good."

He said, "It doesn't matter how it looks, it matters whether or not you do it. You don't have to put this picture on a public bulletin board. We're not going to publish it in the paper. It's just for you to look at, to see where you are and where you are going financially." And I offer to you that advice. It's not important that I know how you're doing. It's not important that anyone else knows how you're doing. But it is desperately important that you know how you're doing. If you're making progress, not making progress, on track, or off track.

When Mr. Shoaff said, "Let's take a picture," I was really embarrassed. *Liabilities?* I had plenty of liabilities. I owed my parents and others. I added all of it. *Assets?* I'm really embarrassed. I'm scraping the bottom of the barrel, even put my shoes on the list. Anything I could think of to make me look a little better. After all, the Salvation Army would probably give me $2 for my shoes.

Then Mr. Shoaff said, "Now, Mr. Rohn, whether or not this financial statement looks the same next year depends on whether or not you change."

So I started this whole process of change. Transform your ability to have the kind of future you have always wished for.

THE STARTING LINE

Now let me give you the numbers. The following is what I ask kids: "What should you do with a dollar?" How many philosophies do you suppose there are about what a child should do with a dollar? You can't believe how many there are. One philosophy is: "He's just a kid, and it's only a dollar. What difference could it possibly make?" Wow, what an error in judgment. Where do you think economics starts? It starts with a child and a dollar.

Another incorrect philosophy, "Let the child spend it all." When would you hope his being a child would stop? When he's 50 and broke, and then he'll learn something? No, no, no. Don't wait to learn how to put wise financial decisions into practice—start children early to be wise financially. And if you need to get back on track, start now.

So if a child wants to spend the whole dollar, persuade him or her not to spend the whole dollar.

He may say, "Why not? It's my dollar." Your response needs to be, "I know it's your dollar, and I know you earned it, but don't spend it all. And I'll show you why." Kids learn best visually. So, put him in your car and drive to the other side of town. Show them where people live who spend the whole dollar—they will get the message. Ask, "Would you like to live here where people spend the whole dollar?" The answer will be no.

And if you already live there, then just show the kid around the neighborhood and tell him how you are making changes to improve your current financial circumstances. Then, show him how to make the changes, too. Show your children how to dynamically affect their lives with a few simple disciplines practiced every day and not neglected. Everyone can walk away from the ghetto, can walk away from welfare, and can walk away from wherever they are. Walk out into the sunlight, and your life can take on whole new dimensions of power, prosperity, and all the rest of what is valuable and unique.

I'm going to share a formula with you that drastically transformed my life. I've been teaching it to teenagers and adults alike for almost 20 years. I want to share it with you because I want this to be a special day—one you will never forget.

THE NUMBERS

Never spend more than 70 cents out of every dollar from now on.

If you need to get back on a solid financial track, start now.

When I met Mr. Shoaff, I was spending about 110 percent of every dollar. That's ruinous. If your outgo exceeds your income, your upkeep becomes your downfall. That's a good little scenario to remember. So the number I found that works best in developing a good financial plan is 70 percent.

What do you do with the remaining 30 cents? My best advice is to give 10 cents (10 percent) to a charity that is supporting worthy projects, helping people who can't help themselves. Some churches teach tithing, which is returning a portion of what you take out. And nothing teaches children responsibility and character better than generosity. No school, no class, no teacher can teach character better than the simple act of being generousand giving 10 cents out of every dollar to help others.

Of course, you can pick your own numbers. I'm just giving you my best scenario. Now is the time to help your children see the value in giving to charity. Start when the amounts are small, when it's easy for them to give a dime out of a dollar. Kids won't mind giving you 10 cents out of every dollar if it's part of their philosophy, if you sell them on it.

It becomes a little harder to give 100,000 out of 1,000,000. Someone says, "Oh, if I had $1,000,000, I'd give $100,000." I'm not sure about that. Start early when the amounts are small so your philosophy will be settled in your mind when the big amounts start to come.

So, spend no more than 70 percent, and then give 10 percent to charity.

The next 10 cents is to be spent on what I call "active capital." Capital meaning, try to make a profit. We live in a capitalistic society where people can make a profit by selling something or rendering a service to people.

Capital belongs in the hands of the people, that's where the genius is. I teach kids that profits are better than wages. Wages are okay, and wages help you make a living. But profits help you make a fortune, to become financially independent. The key is to understand philosophically this simple economic scenario, and you'll realize there are all kinds of ways to make a profit.

Should kids pay taxes? In California where I live, kids do pay taxes. If an eight-year-old walks into 7-Eleven and buys something that costs a dollar, the proprietor makes him cough up seven more pennies. The youngster asks, "What's the seven pennies for?" The proprietor says, "Those pennies pay the taxes." Kid says, "Well, I'm only eight." Proprietor says, "Congratulations, you're my youngest taxpayer." So in California, kids do pay taxes. Now the question is, should they? Yes. Of course.

If an 8-year-old wants to ride his bicycle on the sidewalk instead of in the mud, taxes have to be paid to pay for the sidewalk. Aircraft carriers keep tyranny away from our nation's shores. Aircraft carriers cost money. It's expensive to run a nation, states, communities, and schools.

So back to the 10 percent for active capital and trying your best to show a profit.

There are many ways to show a profit, not just generating financial income. When you touch something and leave it better than you found it, that's a profit. Some profits are intangible. Some profits are tangible. Long before "Earth Day," it was proper and common sense to turn off the lights when you left your hotel room. Why? To conserve energy, to leave a profit. Someone says, "Well, the hotel gets the profit." What do you care? All you need to become is a person who leaves a profit—who does the right thing.

I talked to a man who runs a whole string of apartments. He said, "Guess what? Most people, when they rent an apartment, leave it trashed, worse than they found it." What kind of reputation is that? A rotten one. That's a poor philosophy that leads to poverty. Small lives. As one writer wrote of these types of people, "Living lives of quiet desperation." This is where it all begins. Failure to leave a profit when you can, turn off the lights, pick up and toss into the bin a piece of trash along the way. It doesn't matter what it is, become profit-minded. Profits are better than wages, because profit has the potential to make a fortune. Wages have the potential to make a living.

So I teach kids to take part of the wages they earn and give 10 percent for charity and 10 percent to try and make a profit. For example, I teach kids how to have two bicycles, one to ride and one to rent. It doesn't take long to get into business. You don't have to be a genius. Anyone even halfway bright can start showing a profit.

70, 10, 10, 10

So to recap, I teach kids and adults alike not to spend more than 70 percent. Then 10 percent for charity, 10 percent for active capital and 10 percent for passive capital.

The 10 cents for "passive capital" means letting somebody else use the capital. You provide it, you're passive. They're active, and they pay you interest to use your money. There is profit in charging interest, and this is a unique way to make a fortune.

In fact, I teach teenagers this Bible philosophy that says, *"the borrower is servant to the lender."*[2] There is power in being a lender. Let somebody else use your capital.

Some projects require more capital than any one person has, so there are capital "pools," whether you put it in a financial institution (bank, credit union, etc.). Earn interest, earn a profit, buy a car and sell it for more than you paid for it. Why? Because you leave it better than you found it. Touch something and leave a profit and gain a profit. Profit is not always wrapped up in money and economics. This helps you visualize other ways to use your profit and capital and expenditures, what to do with your time and your life as well as what to do with your money.

These scenario examples are the ideal. What's important is to set up the ideal and work toward it.

At first, you may not be able to do these exact 70, 10, 10, 10 numbers. Some people are in such a desperate situation that currently they are working with 97, 1, 1, 1. That's where I had to start. Start with pennies. Start right where you are. And remember, it's not the amount that counts, it's the discipline, the habit you are establishing. Mr. Shoaff made it clear to me, saying, "It's not the amount that counts, it's the plan that counts."

I told Earl Shoaff, "If I had more money, I'd have a better plan."

He said, "No, Mr. Rohn. If you had a better plan, you'd have more money." It's not the money, it's not the amount, it's the plan that counts. So set up an ideal plan for yourself.

THE IDEAL PLAN

You can rearrange the plan and modify it to suit your particular circumstances. I'm just giving you examples. So set up the ideal and then start making progress toward it, because finally, these numbers are going to change when you move up into the higher numbers.

The people I work with around the world couldn't spend 70 cents out of every dollar, it would be obscene. It would be too much. So the numbers are bound to change. I don't know what mine are right now, but I spend about 20 percent and give a lot larger percentages to charity and active and passive capital. The numbers can change the more financial growth you experience. I'm offering you a good, flexible philosophy and discipline that will serve you well throughout your years.

Remember, philosophy is the set of the sail. The economy is not the set of the sail for you. For you, the set of the sail is your own philosophy, your own thinking, your own plan, your own concept. Don't borrow somebody else's plan. Don't borrow somebody else's concept. Don't borrow the concept of, "Spend all you can, cross your fingers, and hope for the best." Don't borrow that. Develop your own philosophy, and it will lead you to unique places.

STRICT ACCOUNTING

One of the best disciplines is to keep strict financial accounts. Did you ever hear or ever say this expression concerning money: "I don't know where it all goes? It just gets away from me." Don't let that become your philosophy. Keep track of all your financial transactions. Ensure your money is being recorded accurately. This is important.

A POSITIVE FINANCIAL ATTITUDE

Next, develop a new attitude as well as new concepts. I used to say, "I hate to pay my taxes."

Mr. Shoaff said, "Well, that's one way to live."

I said, "Well, doesn't everybody hate to pay their taxes?"

He said, "No, a lot of us are way past that attitude. Once you understand what taxes are, that taxes are part of our governmental system, our society. Taxes are used to care for and feed the goose that lays the golden eggs—democracy and liberty and freedom. Free enterprise. Don't you want to feed the goose that lays the golden eggs?"

Somebody says, "Well, the goose eats too much." That's probably true. I understand that. But better a fat goose than no goose. And here's the truth, we all eat too much. Let not one appetite accuse another. Of course, the government needs to go on a diet. So do most of us. But hey, you still have to care for and feed the goose. When you understand that, you will have the right attitude.

I used to say, "I hate to pay my bills."

Mr. Shoaff said, "Well, that's one way to live."

I said, "Well, doesn't everybody hate to pay their bills?"

He said, "No. Some of us are way beyond that. Next time you pay $100 on an account, put a little note in there and say, 'With great delight, I send you this $100.' They don't get many letters like that. When you reduce your liabilities and increase your assets, you will see your picture changing, your financial statement improving. I love to pay my bills, keep the money in circulation, pay my taxes, and feed the goose that lays the golden eggs. It's a matter of attitude."

And the last piece of advice on attitude—everybody must pay. Life is full of opportunity, but life also costs a price—a price we must all pay. We must all share. One of the classic stories of all time from ancient Bible script says that one day, Jesus and His disciples were standing by the synagogue, watching people as they came by and put their offering in the treasury. Some people came by and put in large amounts. Others put in modest amounts, average amounts.

And the story says that "a poor widow came by and dropped in two small coins. 'I tell you the truth,' Jesus said, 'this poor widow has given more than all the rest of them. For they have given a tiny part of their surplus, but she, poor as she is, has given everything she has.'"[3] Wow, what a lesson to learn. It's not the amount, it's what it represents of your life that counts.

Now let me give you the wisdom of the scenario that did *not* occur, which may teach us even more. Jesus did *not* reach into the treasury and get out this widow lady's two pennies and run after her saying, "Here, little lady, My disciples and I have decided that you're so pitiful and you're so poor that we want to give you back your two pennies." I'm telling you that did *not* occur.

If Jesus had done that, she would've been insulted. And rightfully so. She may have said in response, "I know my two pennies aren't much, but it represented most of what I had. And you insult me by not letting me contribute what I wanted to contribute, even if it's only two pennies."

Jesus left her pennies in the treasury, meaning everybody has to pay, even if it's only pennies. That's the key. And whether you start with pennies or whether you start with dollars or whether you start with nothing, remember that part of the scenario is to spend, of course. Part of the scenario is to invest, and part of the scenario is to show a profit. And part of the scenario is to help take care of people who can't take care of themselves.

Set up your own philosophy that will take you where you want to go. I'm not asking you to buy my philosophy or adopt my specific numbers. I only want to provoke you to think, for you to come up with a splendid economic philosophy that will wake you up early and keep you up late, because you are thinking and pondering ways to use your resources and turn them into the dreams you want for the future.

And that's my proven-successful advice to you on financial independence.

NOTES

1. Matthew 6:24 NLT.

2. Proverbs 22:7 NLT.

3. Luke 21:2-4 NLT.

8

WORDS CAN WORK MIRACLES

The last subject to consider when choosing to have your best year ever is communication—how to affect other people with words. I've have developed a four-point teaching that will energize your growth, boost your production, and ensure your happiness. Some of the most important skills parents can learn, teachers can learn, colleagues can learn, all of us can learn, is how to touch and affect other people with the power and uniqueness of words.

Communication is so important that words can actually work miracles. Words are powerful. Words are almost Godlike; in fact, ancient script says, *"The Word was with God, and the Word was God."*[1] Wow. I said to my Israeli audience last year, *"In the beginning....Jehovah God said, 'Let there be light,' and there was light."*[2] The story of creation is unique—words created light. Is that possible? I'm telling you it's possible.

Humans can get pretty close to creating light with their words. For example, what if someone can't possibly see how he or she could do well, become successful, could transform their life and their health, their future and their finances, spiritually

Words can
work miracles.

and every other way? This person can't see, and you come along and share your story, and maybe borrow some other stories. And by the time you get through with a good presentation to this person, he says, "Now I can see! Before you started speaking to me, I was blind. I was in the dark. And while you were talking, so many opportunities dawned on me!"

Is it possible to create light with human intelligence with words? The answer is yes, of course.

Here's part of the spectacular opportunity we have as human beings, one person talking to, communicating with another. Conversations have so much power, so much potential. A mother talking to a daughter, a father talking to a son, a salesperson talking to a client. There is nothing more powerful and awe-inspiring than words, which have the ability to dramatically affect people's lives and futures.

So become a good communicator—your words can benefit all involved.

FOUR STEPS TO GOOD COMMUNICATION

The following are four excellent keys to effective and useful communication.

1. HAVE SOMETHING GOOD TO SAY.

Communication starts with preparation, getting ready to speak to others individually or in groups. Attend classes, read books, have something good to say to people. Here are four good words to help you to have something good to say: interest; fascination; sensitivity; and knowledge. Let's look at each of these four good words one at a time.

Interest. Develop a new interest in people and life and what's going on, including economics, politics, religion, social structure, possibilities, and opportunities.

Fascination. Develop a fascination that goes a step beyond interest. Fascination is why kids learn so much that first six years. Adults walk on ants. Kids get down and study ants—they're fascinated. "How can that ant can carry something way bigger than he is?" Wow. That's why they learn so much, they're fascinated. Another little clue I've learned is to *turn frustration into fascination*. One day, when I was on the freeway in Los Angeles and my plane was leaving in 45 minutes, the traffic was moving not one inch. I am fascinated. Now, this tactic doesn't work every time, but every time it does work, you'll come away with more. Learn to be fascinated instead of frustrated, if you possibly can. Turn that little scenario on for yourself.

Sensitivity. To be your best at communicating with people, you have to understand where they are coming from, where they've been, and what's going on in their lives. Sensitivity training is so important. People are not like you. People have various challenges and problems and difficulties. Do your best to be sensitive to other people when they find themselves in a pit. Be sensitive to that situation. Two of the greatest things said about Jesus: One, He was compassionate. He was touched and moved by what people were experiencing. If you really want to communicate well, be touched and moved, not just by your own drama of life, but by the drama you know is going on in other people's lives.

For example, how does an adult talk to a child? One of the best ways to identify with a child who's 12 and you're 40 is to remember when you were that age. Go back. Remember the scenario and let it hit you again. Let it touch you again. I remember almost every day of being 12. I mean, if I heard it once, I heard it 100 times, "Of course, you can't go. You're not a teenager." And I would think, *Wow, I can't wait for this year to be finished.* Remembering is part of sensitivity.

Saul from Tarsus was a hater and killer of Christians. After he was converted, he became a leader; he became Paul the revered apostle. Why was he so effective in his language and his ability to touch people with his words and with his presence? Because he remembered the dark pit where he came from.

What makes a good performance, a good actor? Emotion close to the surface and then well-chosen words delivered with powerful passion.

Knowledge. You will have something good to say when you take notes of life and gather that wisdom and knowledge into your journal. Gather knowledge from your library and what other credible people have to say on cassettes and videos and other means. Gather knowledge. Don't be lazy in learning. A major part of communication is preparation—be prepared to say something good, interesting, and fascinating.

2. SAY IT WELL.

The next part of good communication is to say it well. One is having something good to say, and number two is to say it well. Let me give you a quick list on saying it well. The best place to start if you want to communicate well is to let your *sincerity* show. Next is *repetition.* Repeat what you have to say so it sticks with the listener. But don't repeat so much that they tune you out. Next, *brevity.* Sometimes, you don't need many words if you're totally sincere, which of course you are. Sometimes, in fact, many times, just a few words could be dynamic in affecting someone else's life—a child, a business colleague, a friend, a sales client.

To say it well, you need to build an excellent vocabulary. Some of my friends took a survey among prisoners in a rehabilitation program. They weren't particularly looking for this, but here's what they found. There's definitely a relationship between vocabulary and behavior. The more limited the vocabulary, the more tendency toward poor behavior. And when you think about it for a while, it makes sense. Words are a way of seeing, and if you don't have a good vocabulary, you can't see very well. Can you imagine the mistakes in judgment when you can't see very well?

Words express what's going on in your head and in your heart.

Next, words express what's going on in your head and what's going on in your heart. What if you can't see well and you can't express well? The result would be a tragic scenario of 5, 10, 20 years of showing no improvement. Then, behavior becomes a major problem, and that person's world gets smaller and smaller. Why? They don't see and they can't express themselves. And finally, they don't need a much bigger place than a 10- by 12-foot cell. Their world is so small anyway, that they don't need a bigger place. I'm asking you to stretch your vocabulary. I used to write words on a 3 by 5 card and post it in my car. I drove a lot back in those days, and at the end of each day, I had learned two or three new words and their meanings.

My oldest daughter, Linda, and my young grandkids start the day with a "word for the day." Linda writes a word on the chalkboard, and the kids memorize the word and the meaning. Then, every once in a while during the day, she says, "What's the word for the day?" And they answer her correctly. The last day I was visiting one time, the word was "superficial." Linda asked Natalie, who was four, "What's the word of the day?" Natalie answered, "Superficial." Then Linda asked Nathaniel, who was five, "What does superficial mean?" He answered, "On the surface." That communication happened several times during the day. If you were to ask my grandkids, "The last time Grandpa was here, what was the word for the day?" I'll bet you they'd probably know. "Superficial, on the surface."

Why not add to your vocabulary so you can see more, see better, and express better. Put out in words what's in your heart, what's in your soul, what's in your mind. Communication is important in every area of your life; so, *say it well, have something good to say,* and *read your audience.* These are simple concepts that mean a lot in getting along with people and having your best day, week, month, and year ever. You have to add some of the details, but that's what I'm mainly good for—concepts.

3. READ YOUR AUDIENCE.

If you're talking to a child, you have to study the child's face and body language. Study what's going on so you know whether to shift gears, come on a little stronger or ease off a little, or search for another illustration. A lot of good communication is dictated by reading your audience. When I first started lecturing, I had some challenges. I was so absorbed in my notes that the audience could have left and I would have kept right on talking. I didn't know how to read my audience.

Read your audience by what you see, **what you hear,** and what you feel.

So always read your audience, whether a prospect, a group, or anyone you speak to.

There are a three different ways to read your audience—by what you see, hear, and feel. *Read what you see* means noticing a person's body language, which tells you when to shift gears, whether to go on, and whether to stop. If you're talking to somebody and they are leaning toward the door, that means you should hurry because they are ready to leave. If a guy's arms are folded and his chin is tucked downward, he is going to be a tough sell. You have your work cut out for you, so reach deep into your bag. Find some extraordinary stories to tell. If someone is leaning toward you and looks relaxed and is listening, enjoy the interaction.

The next way to read your audience is to *read what you hear.* When speaking with children, they don't mind telling you when they're bored or impatient. A kid's attention span is short, so say what you have to say quickly. Adults may say something such as, "Well, that's all very interesting. Thanks for stopping by." That's a strong cue to wrap it up. Read what you hear, and listen for responses. Then you know whether to shift gears, change your language, or find a new illustration.

Another way to read your audience is to *read what you feel.* Women are probably better at this than men when it comes to picking up emotional signals. In general, men can see and can hear, but it takes a little training for a man to feel emotional signals, which are so important to keep you from saying something insensitive. It's so easy to make a mistake in language. For example, if you meant to say to someone you care about, "What's troubling you?" And instead you say, "What's wrong with you?" the person hears a totally different and insensitive attitude. So read the emotional signals, how the person seems to be feeling.

Women seem to have a built-in sensitivity toward others, especially danger. Way back, the man was the provider and the woman was the protector at home, so she could detect danger more quickly. Take, for instance, two scenarios: 1) In the middle of the night, when the baby cries, mama wakes up, papa sleeps. The faintest cry and mama's awake. 2) At night, the wife nudges her husband and says, "Go look around. Something isn't right." He mumbles, "What do you mean it isn't right? Everything's okay." She says, "Go look." He says, "Okay," and he gets out of bed, goes downstairs, and sees that the front door is open. How did she know that? We don't know. She just knows, she knows. It's so valuable in good communication to be able to pick up emotional signals as well as what you see and what you hear.

Ancient scenario says that there are shepherds and sheep and wolves. And some wolves are so clever they dress up like sheep to deceive people.[3] Man says, "Looks like a sheep, talks like a sheep. Must be a sheep." Woman says, "That's no sheep. Take my word for it, I can tell." They know. Read, the signals. Don't ignore them. Develop this personal development scenario. Communication, financial independence, and all the rest.

4. INTENSITY.

The fourth strategy to communicating well is to speak with intensity. Use words mixed with emotion, words mixed with hate, words mixed with love. Words mixed with faith, words mixed with courage. Those types of words make

Put more of **you** into what you say.

communication powerful. Words have a certain effect, but words loaded with emotion have an incredible effect.

My best advice about communication to share with you? Put more of you into what you say. Don't be casual in language, in your words. Casualness leads to casualties in communication. Don't be lazy in learning good communication.

A caution: Measure the intensity of your emotion according to the occasion. In leadership training, we teach not to shoot a cannon at a rabbit. It's effective, but there's no more rabbit. That's a powerful scenario for understanding effective communication. Good communication is using well-chosen words mixed with measured emotion that will positively affect people.

And one last point on communication—*the more you care, the stronger you can be.* The more you care as a

Good communication is using well-chosen words mixed with measured emotion **that will positively affect people.**

mother, the stronger you can be for your children. The more you care as a father, the stronger you can be for your family. The more you care as a leader, the stronger you can be in helping to solve problems. But you have to care. I don't mind the minister consigning my soul to hellfire for my sinful ways as long as he does it with tears, not joy. You can't legitimately preach hellfire unless your heart breaks. Otherwise it's a performance.

Some conversations don't make sense unless they're accompanied by tears. It doesn't mean anything unless accompanied by a broken heart. Learn to speak with measured emotions for the occasion. Remember, draw from well-chosen words and an expanded vocabulary. Be interesting and fascinating. Pull all this together, and your ability to touch other people will grow day by day, week by week, month by month, and year by year.

My last subject comes in two parts—*learn how to cry well and laugh well*. First is the negative part—there wouldn't be positive without negative—both are part of the life scenario. An ancient script says it best, *"For everything there is a season...a time to cry and a time to laugh."*[4] And you have to be wise enough to know when it's a time to cry and not to laugh.

How can you identify with people if you don't cry with them when they are crying? Negative times in life are normal. You must learn to handle each negative time that lands on your doorstep. You can't dismiss it, and don't ignore it. Let it be part of your scenario. Learn to master the tough times—they make us better than we are to wrestle with them the next time.

Times of trouble make us better than we are because they move us to be alert to tyranny, ignorance, or procrastination

Learn how to cry well and laugh well.

that rob us of our fortune or health. You have to do battle with the enemies outside and inside. So learn how to handle the negative.

So there is a time to cry and a time to laugh—to be positive. There will come the day, and many days, that turn your life around.

TURN YOUR LIFE AROUND

There are actually four parts to the day that turn your life around disgust, decision, desire, and resolve.

1. DISGUST

Disgust is a negative emotion, but it can have a very positive, powerful effect. Disgust says, "I've had it." What an important day that could be. How can that be? A company in New York invited me to come and speak. There, I met a beautiful, powerful, accomplished executive lady who was the vice president. I got to know her and asked her about her story. "How did you get here? "She had a large income, yet never attended college. She said, "Well, let me tell you part of the scenario. When I was a young mother a few years ago, one day, I asked my husband for ten dollars. And he said, 'What for?'"

Then she said, "Before that day was over, I decided I would never ever ask again."

She paused, then continued, "I started studying opportunity and found it. I took classes, put myself through school, and now I'm vice president. I make a lot of money. I kept my promise to myself. I've never ever had to ask for money again."

That is called a life-changing day. The day you say enough is enough now, never again. If you can add an act to your disgust, it helps. A man takes a shotgun to his car, blows out every window, destroys every tire, puts a hundred rounds in it, and says, "I've driven this embarrassing thing for the last time." And then he keeps it. Later, when somebody says, "How did you become rich and powerful?" he says, "Let me show you this car. One day, I was so disgusted that I blew it to smithereens." Enough is enough. Powerful.

2. DECISION

Decision-making is a life-changing day. If, in the next few days, you wrote down a list of wise decisions, it could furnish enough inspiration for the next 5 to 10 years. What an inspiring day, the day you can bring yourself to decide to take action, you decide to make that choice you have been putting off, you decide to make that move, you decide to take advantage of the opportunity that's been sitting on the shelf or in the filing cabinet.

3. DESIRE

Desire is wanting something bad enough to get it. Who knows the mystery of that? We don't know. But something I do know is that sometimes, desire waits for a trigger, waits for something to happen. Who knows what the happening may be. A song, the lyrics, a movie, some obscure dialogue, a seminar, sermon, book, an experience, confrontation with an enemy, a conversation with a friend who finally levels with you. Whatever the experience is, it's so valuable to stir up desire. My best advice? Welcome all experiences. You never know which one is going to turn on everything and turn your day around.

Don't put up walls to keep out disappointment, to keep out happiness. Take down all the walls. Go for the experience, the opportunities, the hurts and the happiness. Let each moment teach you.

4. RESOLVE

Resolve says "I will!" which are two of the most powerful words in the language. Prime Minister of the United Kingdom Benjamin Disraeli said, "Nothing can resist a human will that will stake its existence on its purpose." Shortly put, I'll do it or die. The best definition of resolve is one from a junior high girl in Foster City, California. One day, I asked the kids, "Who can tell me what resolve means?" The young girl about three rows back said, "I think I know, Mr. Rohn. I think resolve means promising yourself that you will never give up." That's the best I've ever heard.

I want you to resolve, to promise yourself to never give up. Resolve to read the books until your skills change. Resolve to go to seminars until you get a handle on what you need to learn. Resolve to listen until it makes sense. Resolve you

Resolve means
promising yourself to never give up.

will go for it until you understand it. Resolve you will practice until you develop the skill. Never give up until however long that is. Step by step, piece by piece, book by book, word by word, apple by apple. Walk around the block—go for it. Don't miss the chance to grow, and resolve to pay the price until you learn, change, and become. Along the way, you will discover many of life's best treasures.

BUILD A LIFE WORTH LIVING

I've learned a lot over the years, and the following are bits and pieces of the wisdom accumulated. In addition to what you have read, I offer each of these to you as building block strategies for growth, productivity, and happiness that will lay a firm foundation for your best year now and years to come.

- Learn to help people with their lives, not just their jobs.
- Learn to help others with what matters.
- Touch people with a book, a poem.
- Touch people with some encouraging words.
- Don't fail to listen.
- Help people set their goals.
- Help them with their dreams.
- Help them see what the future can be.
- Help them through their errors and mistakes.
- Take your role as a parent seriously. Being a parent is the most important role you have.

- Help your kids with their lives, not just their homework.

- Help your kids grow into happy, productive, and bright adults.

- Develop good communication.

- Set goals and strive to achieve each one.

- Appreciate and share your gifts, talents, and skills.

Look where my gifts have brought me today—the chance to invest in untold numbers of lives worldwide. Can you imagine what that feels like? I have been given opportunities to choose the best words I could craft and share them with you. I mix my words with my heart and soul and touch people's lives in an effort to help them become the people they were meant to be. It's an awesome experience, and I ask you to work on your gifts too. Your gifts will bring you to a wonderful place for you, an opportunity for you.

And maybe one of these days, people will be reading your book, buying your product, sitting in your seminar, watching you perform, or listening to the story of you becoming powerful, earning, growing, changing, developing, and evolving into your own unique place in the world.

If I have inspired you to that point by what you have read, thank you for giving me the greatest opportunity of investing my life into yours. It's been an awesome experience for me. Thank you and God bless you.

NOTES

1. John 1:1 NLT.

2. Genesis 1:1,3 NLT.

3. Matthew 7:15 NLT.

CONCLUSION

THE NEXT STEP

Congratulations! Simply by reading and absorbing the advice and wisdom presented, you've taken a critical first step toward improving your life, a step others neglect to take. We know that if you get just one great idea from this book, it will be worth many times over the price you paid. Plus, the ideas shared will benefit you for a lifetime.

But will you take the next step? That is the critical question, and the only person who can answer it is you. As any star athlete will tell you, the real power and strength lies in the follow-through. Life sometimes, as it does with all of us, just gets in the way and can crowd out our truest heart's desires. People often start out feeling much as you probably do right now, excited, motivated, dedicated, ready to make the changes they need to make to reach the goals and achieve the dreams they've set forth for themselves.

But it's simply human nature to lose momentum. Very few people have the extraordinary level of discipline it takes to be exclusively self-motivated. The rest of us need ongoing, inter-active, encouragement, support, and motivation to maintain our enthusiasm and really reach our goals. Without that, it can be impossible to remain focused and on track.

Living your best year ever is as simple as following through by reading, learning, and applying these great ideas, strate-gies, and techniques in your life. When you do, you'll see real and significant improvements immediately.

At this moment, while you're feeling inspired, empowered, and most importantly, ready to take action, we at Night-ingale-Conant want you to keep that feeling going today, tomorrow, and for the rest of your life—and use that enthusi-asm to create the life of your dreams, but we know that's not always easy to do.

So, we share with you a simple yet extremely effective secret to help you to maintain the motivation you're feeling right now, and really achieve the goals that first inspired you to buy and read this book.

This extremely helpful online tool is a *Personal Mis-sion Statement Builder*. In just five short minutes, this free, easy-to-use online service reveals a detailed, clearly defined printed statement of your life's mission, giving you the power to truly accomplish any goal—spiritual, personal, or financial. Your mission statement can be a guiding light, keeping you focused on what's important, the person you're becoming, the life you dream of, and the goals you plan to achieve so your life unfolds exactly the way you want it to.

Use this free service now and you will immediately propel yourself toward the achievement of your goals and dreams. We know this to be true because thousands of people have already taken this opportunity and experienced rapid and dramatic life transformations as a result. This is your invitation to be next.

If you are committed to having more, doing better, living life to the absolute fullest, and you want to achieve those goals in record time, simply visit our website at www.nightingale.com/missionstatement to begin the process.

Then, look forward to having your best year ever!

ABOUT JIM ROHN

(1930-2009)

For more than 40 years, Jim Rohn honed his craft like a skilled artist—helping people the world over sculpt life strategies that expanded their imagination of what is possible. Those who had the privilege of hearing him speak can attest to the elegance and common sense of his insights and wisdom.

So it is no coincidence that he is still widely regarded as one of the most influential thinkers of our time, and thought of by many as a national treasure. He authored numerous books and audio and video programs and helped motivate and shape an entire generation of personal development trainers and hundreds of executives from America's top corporations.

THANK YOU FOR READING THIS BOOK!

If you found any of the information helpful, please take a few minutes and leave a review on the bookselling platform of your choice.

BONUS GIFT!

Don't forget to sign up to try our newsletter and grab your free personal development ebook here:

soundwisdom.com/classics

Because Your Success Matters

Embark on a transformative journey with Jim Rohn's *The Art of Exceptional Living*. This succinct guide, segmented into focused chapters, offers invaluable insights on personal development, goal setting, and forging a unique path in life. Rohn, with his personal and often humorous anecdotes, encourages readers to evaluate their lifestyles, urging them to become the best versions of themselves. A book that promises not just wealth, but an enrichment of life's value, steering you towards a fulfilling path of self-betterment and happiness. Start living exceptionally today with Rohn's profound wisdom.

Discover the transformative power of true ambition with Jim Rohn's groundbreaking book, *The Power of Ambition*. Rohn, a revered authority on success, guides you on a path to harnessing your innermost drive to foster personal achievement and uplift those around you. Through six pioneering strategies, you'll learn to cultivate a disciplined and eager desire that propels you toward your goals while serving others. From mastering resilience to effective networking, this comprehensive guide is a masterclass in building a life filled with passion and purpose.

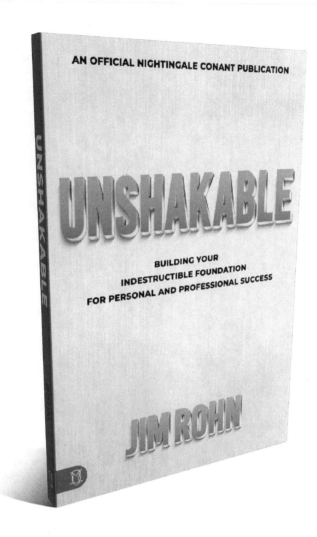

Unlock your potential and pave the road to personal and professional success with *Unshakable*, the famous tour de force from the distinguished Jim Rohn. Drawing from over four decades of insights into human behavior, Rohn presents twelve fundamental qualities to forge an unshakable character that magnetizes success. With captivating insights and actionable strategies, it's your indispensable companion in crafting a rewarding future grounded in steadfast principles. Take the first step towards becoming *Unshakable* — a version of yourself that is grounded, resilient, and primed for success in all life's avenues.

GET ALL 3 BOOKS
AND TAKE CONTROL
OF <u>YOUR</u> LIFE!